THE
BEAUTIFUL NECESSITY

DECORATING WITH
ARTS AND CRAFTS

THE BEAUTIFUL NECESSITY

DECORATING WITH ARTS AND CRAFTS

BRUCE SMITH & YOSHIKO YAMAMOTO

GIBBS·SMITH
P
PUBLISHER

SALT LAKE CITY

ABOUT THE COVER AND FRONT MATTER PHOTOGRAPHS
FRONT COVER PHOTOGRAPH: The "Thistle" wallpaper pattern as produced by Bradbury and Bradbury. PHOTOGRAPH, PAGE 9: A matte-green vase by Roycroft Potters.
BACK COVER PHOTOGRAPH: The carpet is currently made by JAX Rugs.

First Paperback Edition
08 07 06 05 04   5 4 3 2 1

Text © 1996 Bruce Smith and Yoshiko Yamamoto

Published by
Gibbs Smith, Publisher
P.O. Box 667
Layton, Utah 84041

orders: 1.800.748.5439
www.gibbs-smith.com

Printed and bound in Korea

Library of Congress Cataloging-in-Publication Data

Smith, Bruce, 1950–
      The beautiful necessity: decorating with arts and crafts / Bruce Smith and Yoshiko Yamamoto. —1st ed.
        p.   cm.
        ISBN 0-87905-778-5; 1-58685-431-3 pbk.
1. Arts and crafts movement—United States. 2. Decorative arts—United States—History—20th century. 3. Interior Decoration—United States—History—20th century. I. Yamamoto, Yoshiko. II. Title.
NK1141.S64 1996
747' .9—dc20   95-45902
                                              CIP

To Vicki and George, we dedicate our labor as here enclosed with thanks and gratitude for abiding us and encouraging us and giving without reservation of home and love and many a good meal.

CONTENTS

The living room of the Gamble House in Pasadena, California.

PREFACE

THE DESIGNER Charles Ashbee wrote that the main issue of the Arts and Crafts movement is "one of production…not so much how things should be made, but what is the meaning behind their making." We have tried, in this book, to look at not just the object, not just the home interior, not just the wallpaper design or the spindles or slats of a chair—we have rather hoped to invest in the book a bit of the meaning behind these objects, behind their design and making, behind the reason for their existence. We have tried, in other words, to look less at the object and more at the craft, less at the product and more at the process.

Often called the birthplace of the Arts and Crafts movement, the 1859 Red House was designed by Philip Webb, architect and close friend of William Morris. Morris and his friends painstakingly furnished the home. After layering bricks and cutting lumber to make the skeleton of the house, Morris realized that it needed well-made and well-designed furnishings. His biographer later wrote, "Not a chair, table, nor bed; not a cloth nor paper hanging for the walls; nor tiles to line fireplaces or passages; not a curtain nor candle-stick; nor a jug to hold wine nor a glass to drink it out of, but had to be reinvented."

We do not see this movement as a passion long gone and dead; we believe it to be well and alive today—all one must do is take a look at the great numbers of people across the nation who are choosing to live a more moderate, reasoned lifestyle—a simpler life, in order to pursue their craft. In our resource list, we have listed as many of these craftspeople as we could find, and where appropriate, we have used examples of their work in the text. For examples of the homes and interiors of the movement, since that is what this book is all about, we have as often as possible provided pictorial examples of homes that are open to the public. We do this fully realizing that, though a picture is worth a thousand words, there is no substitute for the actual experience of the space. We encourage our readers to search out these houses open to the public so as to have the experience of the unfolding of space as one enters Frank Lloyd Wright's Robie House, or the pure aesthetic beauty of sunlight pouring through the stained-glass front door of the Gamble House. Again, in the resource listings in the back of this book are listed houses built under the influence of the Arts and Crafts movement that are open today to the public.

There will be objections to names and makers of the movement we have left out; we have attempted to be representative rather than inclusive. Our purpose has not been to write a history of the movement but rather to present representative samples of the work as it relates to the home and the interior. There are already good books published that are comprehensive, most notably *The Art That Is Life: The Arts & Crafts Movement in America, 1875–1920,* which unfortunately is out of print. But that not always need be the case.

This book is divided into five primary sections: Space, Surface, Light, Function, and Allusion. *Space,* because it is by space that the bare bones of the structure of the house is formed; space is what envelops us; it is within space that we move and live. Once we have space, we find ourselves surrounded by *Surface:* the floors, walls, and ceilings that give visual and tactile reference to our lives. *Light* is always the great forgotten element of the home. It seems invisible, yet without it, all is for naught. The elements that *Function* in the house are what give it life: the furniture, the plumbing, the kitchen hardware. Without these elements we have a body without a life. Finally, because we are human, we need to understand who we are. We read history to understand our present; we take photographs to remember our past. In our homes, we surround ourselves with references to both our present and our past—family photographs and knickknacks, inherited teacups and passed-down quilts. We choose a wallpaper because it gives us reference to a more natural world than we live in at present, or we keep the wood walls unpainted as a reminder to live plainly and simply. *Allusion* is the way that once we have breathed life into a house, we give it a spirit, we make it our own.

A CHRONOLOGY

1876 • The Centennial Exposition is held in Philadelphia.
      • Alexander Graham Bell invents the telephone.

1877 • Edison invents the phonograph.

1878 • A. A. Pope manufactures the first bicycles in America.

1879 • Associated Artists is founded in New York City by Louis Comfort Tiffany, Candace Wheeler, Lockwood de Forest, and Samuel Colman.

1880 • Rookwood Pottery is established in Cincinnati, Ohio.
      • First practical electric lights are developed, and New York's streets are lit by electric lights.

1883 • First skyscraper is built.

1886 • Glessner House in Chicago is built.
      • In Paris, the last exhibition of impressionist paintings is exhibited.

1888 • Arts and Crafts Exposition Society is organized in London.
      • The Guild of Handicraft is founded in London by Charles Ashbee.
      • Jane Addams and Ellen Gates Starr visit Toynbee Hall.

1889 • Hull House is founded by Jane Addams and Ellen Gates Starr in Chicago.
      • The Eiffel Tower is built in Paris.
      • *A Connecticut Yankee in King Arthur's Court,* by Mark Twain, is published.
      • Frank Lloyd Wright builds his home in Oak Park, Illinois. He continues working on it until he leaves for Europe with his mistress in 1909.

1890 • William Morris founds the Kelmscott Press.

1891 • *Knight Errant* begins publication in Boston.
      • Chelsea Pottery begins production.
      • Walter Crane tours America, lecturing.

1893 • World's Colombian Exposition opens in Chicago.
      • *The Studio* begins publication in England.
      • Charles and Henry Greene begin their architectural practice in Pasadena.
      • Frank Lloyd Wright leaves Louis Sullivan's office to establish his own practice in Chicago.
      • Irving Gill moves from Chicago to San Diego to establish his own practice.
      • John Bradstreet establishes his crafts center of carvers, gilders, painters, and furniture makers in Minneapolis, Minnesota.

1894 • Elbert Hubbard visits the Kelmscott Press in England, possibly meeting William Morris.
      • Grueby Pottery begins production.
      • Swedenborgian Church is built in San Francisco.

1895 *The Time Machine,* by H. G. Wells, is published.
      • The motion-picture camera is invented.
      • America's first Arts and Crafts society, The Chalk and Chisel Club, is formed in Minneapolis.
      • Newcomb Pottery is founded in New Orleans.
      • Charles Keeler's house is built in Berkeley, California—Bernard Maybeck's first commission.

1896 • Elbert Hubbard begins publication of *The Philistine* at East Aurora, New York. It is published until his death in 1915.
      • The first Roycroft book is published.
      • William Morris dies.
      • Charles Ashbee visits America for the first time.
      • Dedham Pottery begins.
      • The Guild of Arts and Crafts is formed in San Francisco.
      • *House Beautiful* begins publication in Chicago featuring the work of Frank Lloyd Wright.

1897 • The first American Arts and Crafts Exhibition is held in Boston by the Boston Society of Arts and Crafts.
      • The Chicago Arts and Crafts Society is formed at Hull House.
      • The Rochester Arts and Crafts Society is founded.
      • *The International Studio,* the American edition of *Studio,* begins publication.

1898 • Gustav Stickley travels to Europe and, upon return, begins Gustav Stickley & Co. in Syracuse, New York.
      • Henry Chapman Mercer starts Moravian Pottery in Doylestown, Pennsylvania, as a way to preserve the dying pottery craft.
      • Charles Lummis begins building his home, El Alisal, in Highland Park, Los Angeles.
      • Charles Rohlfs opens his Furniture Shop in Buffalo, New York, abandoning a theatrical career.
      • The Hillside Club is founded in Berkeley, California.

1899 • Adelaide Alsop Robineau begins publication of *Keramic Studio* in Syracuse, New York.
   • The Boston Society of Arts and Crafts holds its second exhibition.
   • Gustav Stickley forms United Crafts in Eastwood, a Syracuse, New York, suburb.
   • Chicago's Industrial Art League is formed.

1900 • L. & J. G. Stickley Co. is formed.
   • The Guild of Arts and Crafts is organized in New York.
   • The Minneapolis Handicraft Guild begins.
   • The Arden Community is founded by William Price and others in Arden, Delaware; lasts only one year.
   • Hull House Bookbindery is opened by Ellen Gates Starr.
   • William Day Gates introduces his Teco Line of Pottery.
   • Charles Ashbee makes his second visit to America, visiting Pittsburgh, Cincinnati, St. Louis, and Chicago, where he meets Wright.

1901 • The Pan-American Exposition takes place in Buffalo, New York, where Stickley and McHugh introduce their line of furniture to the public. Also exhibiting are Charles Rohlfs, L. C. Tiffany, Gorham, Grueby, Newcomb Pottery, Volkmar, and Adelaide Robineau. Charles Greene visits the fair on his way to England—his honeymoon trip; gold medals to Grueby, Rookwood, and Tiffany; silver to Tiffany, Newcomb; bronze to Volkmar.

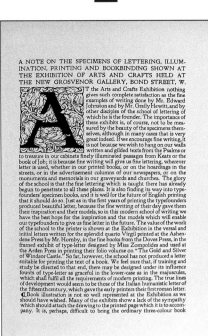

A NOTE ON THE SPECIMENS OF LETTERING, ILLUMINATION, PRINTING AND BOOKBINDING SHOWN AT THE EXHIBITION OF ARTS AND CRAFTS HELD AT THE NEW GROSVENOR GALLERY, BOND STREET, W.

AT the Arts and Crafts Exhibition nothing gives such complete satisfaction as the fine examples of writing done by Mr. Edward Johnston and by Mr. Graily Hewitt, and by other disciples of the school of lettering of which he is the founder. The importance of these exhibits is, of course, not to be measured by the beauty of the specimens themselves, although in many cases that is very great indeed. If we encourage fine writing, it is not because we wish to hang on our walls written and gilded texts from the Psalms or to treasure in our cabinets finely illuminated passages from Keats or the book of Job; it is because fine writing will give us fine lettering, wherever letter is used, whether in our printed books, or on the hoardings in the streets, or in the advertisement columns of our newspapers, or on the monuments and memorials in our graveyards and churches. The glory of the school is that the fine lettering which is taught there has already begun to penetrate to all these places. It is also finding its way into typefounders' specimen books, and it is well for the future of English printing that it should do so. Just as in the first years of printing the typefounders produced beautiful letter, because the fine writing of their day gave them their inspiration and their models, so in this modern school of writing we have the best hope for the inspiration and the models which will enable our typefounders to give us fine letter in the future. The value of the work of the school to the printer is shown at the Exhibition in the versal and initial letters written for the splendid quarto Virgil printed at the Ashendene Press by Mr. Hornby, in the fine books from the Doves Press, in the framed exhibit of type-letter designed by Miss Zompolides and used at the Arden Press in printing their folio volume on "The Gold and Silver of Windsor Castle." So far, however, the school has not produced a letter suitable for printing the text of a book. We feel sure that, if training and study be directed to that end, there may be designed under its influence founts of type-letter as graceful in the lower-case as in the majuscules, which shall fulfil all the requirements of modern printing. The true lines of development would seem to be those of the Italian humanistic letter of the fifteenth century, which gave the early printers their first roman letter.
¶Book illustration is not so well represented at the Exhibition as we should have wished. Many of the exhibits show a lack of the sympathy which should attach the drawing to the printed page which it is to accompany. It is, perhaps, difficult to bring the ordinary three-colour book

• Will Price organizes the Rose Valley Community outside Philadelphia, Pennsylvania.
• Mission Inn in Riverside, California, is opened by Frank Miller.
• *House & Garden* begins publication in Philadelphia.
• *The Craftsman* begins publication in Syracuse, New York.
• Roycroft begins production of furniture.
• Frank Lloyd Wright delivers his lecture "The Art and Craft of the Machine" at Hull House in Chicago.
• Will Bradley begins publication of his "Bradley Houses" in *Ladies' Home Journal*.

1902 • *Handicraft* magazine begins publication by the Boston Society of Arts and Crafts.
   • Ralph Radcliffe Whitehead founds the Byrdcliffe Community, just outside Woodstock, New York.

The term "Arts and Crafts" was coined by the bookbinder T. J. Cobden Sanderson in 1888 when a group of craftsmen and artisans in London, including William Morris, were trying to come up with a name to describe their exhibition society. From then on, the name "Arts and Crafts" came to be adopted by many crafts groups on both sides of the Atlantic.

• Charles Limbert Company is formed.
• Artus van Briggle founds pottery in Colorado Springs, Colorado.
• The Dayton Society of Arts and Crafts is formed in Dayton, Ohio, by Forest Emerson Mann.

1903 • Dard Hunter joins Roycroft.
   • *The Artsman* begins publication at Rose Valley with motto "The Art that Is Life."
   • Harvey Ellis starts work for Gustav Stickley in June of 1903, dies January of 1904, and is buried in a pauper's grave.
   • The Roycroft Inn opens.
   • The Morris Society is started in Chicago.
   • A major exhibition of Arts and Crafts is held at the Craftsman Building in Syracuse.
   • The Craftsman Home Builders Club is formed.
   • *Principles of Home Decoration with Practical Examples,* by Candace Wheeler, is published.

1904 • Louisiana Purchase International Exposition takes place in St. Louis, exhibiting much of the Arts and Crafts work being produced then in America. In the Austrian Pavilion, interiors are presented by Joseph Urban, and the German exhibit is designed by Josef Maria Olbrich.
• Ernest Batchelder moves to California, and his *Principles of Design* is published.
• Charles Keeler's *The Simple Home* is published.
• Gustav Stickley visits California.
• The Marston House is built in San Diego, designed by Irving Gill.
• The Shop of the Crafters in Cincinnati is formed by Oscar Onken.
• Marblehead Pottery begins as part of a craft therapy program but becomes an independent company within a year.
• Robert Riddle Jarvie opens his metalwork shop.

1905 • *The Craftsman* moves to New York.
• Ernest Batchelder visits Ashbee's Guild at Chipping Campden, England, and works in the shops there.
• The Los Angeles Society of Arts and Crafts begins.

1906 • Arthur and Lucia Mathews form the Furniture Shop in San Francisco, starting monthly publication of their magazine, *Philopolis*, and establish the Philopolis Press.

1907 • The National League of Handicrafts, Boston, is formed.

• The Paul Revere Pottery of the Saturday Evening Girls' Club starts to train young girls in craft skills.
• *A Theory of Pure Design: Harmony, Balance, Rhythm*, by Denman Ross, is published.
• The Forest Craft Guild is formed in Grand Rapids, Michigan, by Forest Emerson Mann.

1908 • The Gamble House by Greene and Greene in Pasadena, California, is built.
• The Robie House is built by Frank Lloyd Wright in Chicago.
• Dirk van Erp opens his copper shop in San Francisco.
• Karl Kipp, a former banker, begins work at Roycroft, soon becoming head of the copper shop.
• *The Fra: For Philistines and Roycrofters* begins publication at Roycroft.

1909 • *Craftsman Homes* is published by Stickley.
• The Rose Valley Association goes bankrupt.
• The Arroyo Guild of Craftsmen is formed in Pasadena; only one issue of their *Arroyo Craftsman* magazine is published.
• The William Thorsen House, Berkeley, California, is built, designed by Greene and Greene.
• May Morris, William Morris's daughter, travels to America to lecture on costume and pattern design, embroidery, and jewelry.

• Ernest Batchelder, already a well-known designer, opens his tile company in Pasadena.
• *The Bungalow Magazine* is first published by Henry Wilson in Los Angeles.

1910 • Ernest Batchelder's *Design in Theory and Practice* is published, compiled from articles he wrote for *The Craftsman*.
• First Church of Christ, Scientist, by Bernard Maybeck, is built in Berkeley, California.
• Beaux-Arts Village is founded outside Seattle.

1911 • The Sun House, Ukiah, California, is built.
• Frederick Hurten Rhead organizes a pottery at Arequipa Sanatorium, Fairfax, California.
• Karl Kipp leaves Roycroft to found his own art-metal shop, the Tookay Shop.

1912 • *More Craftsman Homes* is published by Stickley.

1913 • The Grove Park Inn is built in Asheville, North Carolina, furnished by Roycroft. Currently the Grove Park Inn is the site of the annual Arts and Crafts Conference each February.
• Purcell Cutts House in Minneapolis by Purcell and Elmslie, is built.

1914 • The La Jolla Women's Club by Irving Gill is built in La Jolla, California.

1915 • The Lanterman House, La Canada, California, is built.
• On May 7, Elbert Hubbard and his wife Alice die aboard the Lusitania when it is sunk by the Germans.

Entrance Hall of the Glessner House, Chicago, Illinois.

THE AMERICAN BEGINNINGS: THE GLESSNER HOUSE

On the night of May 4, 1886, John and Frances Glessner were reviewing the final drawings for the design of their Chicago home when they were interrupted by a distant explosion—the sound of a bomb going off—followed by gunfire and the yells and screams from crowds. The dynamite explosion, five blocks distant, was the beginning of the Haymarket Riot and Massacre, one of the main incidents in what has been called probably the most violent decade in American history in terms of civil disorders and labor-capital conflicts. The Haymarket bomb was a gauge of what the country was going through: a time of labor turmoil and unrest, of agitation and violence. Elsewhere in the nation, 700,000 workers went on strike, and there were riots against the Chinese. This was a period of vast change in the country—change from the self-employment of craftspeople, printers, carpenters, and cigar makers to the unskilled, hourly work of the factory; change from isolated, self-sufficient, agrarian communities to a society interconnected by telegraph, railroad, and mass marketing—and the change in the society was not going smoothly.

One can see in the rough-hewn, granite massiveness of the exterior façade of the Glessner House a modern counterpart to the security alarm system, a defense against the outside society, against the violence and unrest that come from change. On the inside, however, the U-shape of the house is butted against a wall of the neighbor's property, forming an inner courtyard with a vastly different, friendlier exterior, more in keeping with the rural, formed interior picturesqueness of the quaint

Abingdon Abbey in England. The Abbey's picture was given by the Glessners to their architect, H. H. Richardson, so that he could make it "the key note" of the Glessners' home.

Within this dichotomy of the outer and inner worlds of the Glessner House, one can find a metaphor for the beginnings of the American Arts and Crafts movement: the outer world a protection and reaction against the rapid transformation of society, and an inner world that hearkens back to a more pleasant, bucolic world, English in origin and medieval in nature. Indeed, much of the decoration of the house was English with medieval overtones. There were William Morris floor rugs designed and woven especially for the house, and Morris-designed wallpapers, curtains, and portieres, some of which John Glessner proudly wrote in his description of the house "the most important and typical of which had the pattern drawn on the silk by Mr. Morris's own hand, and much, but not all, of the embroidery done by your mother."

The Sussex chairs of the Morris firm were used by the family, the lamps were hammered by W. A. S. Benson of Morris and Company, and the ceramic tiles, vases, and plates by William DeMorgan were bought through the Morris and Company outlet in a Chicago Department store. The work of Morris and Company had been introduced to America early on, his wallpapers, tiles, curtains, and carpets being sold in a Boston department store as early as 1873. In the Midwest, though, it was the work of Richardson and especially the completeness of the Glessner house interior that brought the work of Morris and Company to view.

Another side of the English movement was transmitted to America by two Chicago women, Jane Addams and Ellen Gates Starr, inspired by a visit to the London settlement house Toynbee Hall less than a year after the Glessners had moved into their house. The idea of Toynbee Hall and the settlement house movement that it hatched was to bring together young Oxford University men with the poor people of London, with resulting benefits to both.

The library of the Glessner House was furnished with carpets and draperies from William Morris and Company.

Wrote the founder of Toynbee Hall about the poor: "It is the poverty of their own life, which makes the poor content to inhabit 'uninhabitable houses.' Such poverty of life can best be removed by contact with those who possess the means of higher life." Beyond providing contact between these disparate classes, the settlement house provided lectures and classes for the uplifting of the poor: courses on the writings of Ruskin, on English history and economics, or classes in carpentry, clay modeling, or woodcarving.

Upon their return from England to Chicago, Addams and Starr began an American version of Toynbee Hall, which they called Hull House, on the edge of a crowded immigrant neighborhood. Their undertaking not only served as a model for other settlement houses across the nation but served as a transmission of the ideas and ideals of the Arts and Crafts movement to the Midwest. It was at Hull House that, in 1897, the Chicago Arts and Crafts Society was founded. And four years later, it was there also that Frank Lloyd Wright gave his famous lecture "The Art and Craft of the Machine." It is there that Charles Ashbee stayed when he came to Chicago, and there that Frances Glessner went to take classes when she wanted to learn the craft of silversmithing.

The beginnings of the Arts and Crafts movement in America were heavily English in style. Inspired by Morris and his followers, they borrowed both the political and social sentiments as well as the imagery. It did not take the nation long, though, to turn the movement into something uniquely its own.

THE SIMPLE HOME

If there is any one difference, beyond the superiority of marketing, to distinguish the English Arts and Crafts movement from the American, one would find it in the concept of the simple home. One of the foremost advocates for simplicity in the home and in one's life was not an American, but a French Protestant minister named Charles Wagner, author of the best-selling book *The Simple Life.* "What material things does a man need to live under the best conditions? A healthful diet, simple clothing, a sanitary dwelling-place, air, and exercise," he wrote.

Inside the Keeler Studio, the open-beamed ceiling and stucco wall are only slightly stained but mostly left in a natural state. The fireplace, though altered from the original, still is supported by the same rough bricks.

"My aim is to point out a direction and tell what advantage would come to each of us from ordering his life in a spirit of simplicity."

The message of simplicity became pervasive throughout the American movement. Gustav Stickley published both writings of and about Wagner's message of simplicity in his magazine *The Craftsman,* and for several years, the subtitle of the magazine was *An Illustrated Monthly Magazine for the Simplification of Life.* One finds other magazines with the same thought: *House Beautiful* publishing articles such as "On the Choice of Simple Furniture," or *House and Garden* on "The Value and Use of Simple Materials in House Building." Frank Lloyd

Wright declared, "Do not think that simplicity means something like the side of a barn, but rather something with a graceful sense of beauty in its utility from which discord and all that is meaningless has been eliminated."

The idea of simplicity was more than an aesthetic judgment; it was part of the movement to reform the household and improve the lot of the housewife. The factories were taking away the servants, and technological improvements were making the lot of the housekeeper easier. Not only was indoor plumbing with running water in wide use, but washing machines and even vacuum cleaners had been invented, too. Frank Lloyd Wright's Robie House of 1908 had a central vacuum system with outlets in each of the rooms, and the Craftsman Farms had an electric dishwasher by 1916 from a company that had been manufacturing them since 1901. In addition, surfaces and spaces were simply easier to clean; two-dimensional decorations, such as stencils, did not gather as much dust as the more traditional plaster frieze.

On the West Coast, the quest for simplicity was most notably advanced by the Berkeley naturalist and poet Charles Keeler. Taking the ferry back and forth to San Francisco, he met the young architect Bernard Maybeck and, finding a kindred soul in the bearded bohemian with the gold cane and cape, he allowed Maybeck to design his home for him. The house, Maybeck's first private commission, was evangelist in nature. Setting the precedent for the simple, wooden style of housing for which Berkeley is known today, it was, as Keeler wrote, a "house of redwood within and without, with all the construction exposed, left in the natural mill-surface finish on the inside and shingled on the outside."

After the house was finished, Keeler, worried that others would "come and build stupid white-painted boxes all around," worked towards planning a "commune" of similar houses on the Berkeley hillside by forming the civic improvement society in 1898 called the Hillside Club. While president of the club from 1903 to 1905, he wrote his paean to simplicity, *The Simple Home,* dedicating it to his good friend Maybeck. Echoing others in the Arts and Crafts movement, he wrote that "the home must suggest the life it is to encompass," and called the home "the family temple." Written as a guide for those who might build nearby, he specified that wood is "generally spoiled by the use of paint or varnish," and stated dictates such as "if color must be used, a creosote shingle stain for the roof, of dull red or a soft warm green, is not apt to destroy the color harmony of the house with reference to the surrounding landscape."

He concluded his writing with the admonition that "of all reforms needed in the life of the home, that of the relation of the man to his family is most pressing. Modern materialism demands of far too many men an unworthy sacrifice. That the wife and children may live in ostentation the man must be a slave to business, rushing and jostling with the crowd in the scramble for wealth. A simpler standard of living will give him more time for art and culture, more time for his family, more time to live."

"Let's have a William Morris afternoon," begins an article in a 1907 issue of *House Beautiful.* "We have been in bondage to these wretched ornaments year after year, and something must be done." One by one, objects are held up, a marble-carved child and dog, Royal Worcester vases, a white china basket covered with china forget-me-nots, and each in turn are judged with the questions: "Does anyone know this to be useful?" and "Now, can any one believe it to be beautiful?" All resoundingly fail to meet the

criteria and are carted up to the attic. All that remain in the living space are "an old brass teapot from Norway, a willow-pattern 'frog' mug over two hundred years old, a small Moki bowl, and a dull brass candlestick. The relief was so great and the result so restful that we sat and feasted our eyes."

ACKNOWLEDGMENTS

The Arts and Crafts movement was a widespread, encompassing movement; thus, a book upon even a facet of the movement needs to draw both deeply and widely. Consequently, while we take full and sole responsibility for whatever mistakes may be in it, we must give much credit and thanks for this book to a number of people and organizations who gave to us of their information and photographs, their resources and time, their encouragement and support.

In particular I would like to give thanks to the following: Michael Adams and Dawn Hopkins; Drake Adkisson of AKA Drake; David Allswang; Laurie King and David Heller of Arroyo Style; The Members of Artistic License for their initial encouragement to stay true to the idea of craft; Michael Ashford; Tim Ashmore and Jill Kessenich of Ashmore/Kessenich Design; Jim Benjamin; Arnold Benetti; Gene Agress, and Kevin Hakman at Berkeley Mills and Furniture; David Berman; Nancy Thomas of Blue Hills Rugs; Ted Bosley who gave of friendship and counsel; Therese Tierney, Bruce Bradbury, and Scott Cazet at Bradbury and Bradbury; Wayne Reckard of Brass Light Gallery; Todd Brotherton; Anthony Bruce at Berkeley Architectural Heritage Association; Tony Smith and Greg Bowman of Buffalo Studios; Micheline Lepine and Nancy Weekly of the Burchfield-Penney Art Center; John Burrows for the cup of tea, the introduction to the John Wingate Weeks Home, and so much more; Sarah Burt and Kevin Oliver; Kitty McCullough at the Byrdcliffe Arts Colony; Terry and Lorna Byrnes; Christine Carr for introducing us to the architecture of Ellsworth Storey, and to Rickard Fick for sharing Ellsworth Storey's home with us; Charlene Casey for an unending supply of enthusiasm; Ann and Andre Chaves with much thanks for always having been willing to give of home and advice; Robert Judson Clark; Nancy Strathern and Suzanne Jones at The Craftsman Farm; Barbara Klein and Melissa Borko at The Craftsman's Guild; Lee Jester at The Craftsman Home; Travis Culwell and Paul Burgin at the College of Environmental Design, University of California, Berkeley; Arnold D'Epagnier; Riley Doty; Paul Duchscherer and Douglas Keister; Thomas Andrews, and Margaret Dickerson at the Historical Society of Southern California in Charles Fletcher Lummis's home, El Alisal; Ron Endlich of Tile Antiques; Michael Fitzsimmons; Greg Foster of Frog Hollow Vermont State Crafts Center; Helen Forster for Maine lobster and a wondrous early morning trip to the Atlantic shore; Judi Benda and Bobbi Mapstone at The Gamble House; Terry Geiser and Janet Mark; John Hamm; Dot Brovarney at the Grace Hudson Museum; David Gray; Austene Hall and Robert Archibald; Linda and Brent Willis of the Handwerk Shop; Thomas Heinz and Ann Terando; David Hellman; Warren and Jillian Hile; Tim Holton and Stephanie McCoy; Rita Hubbard and Ed Godfrey for sharing the wonders of East Aurora with one who freely calls himself a Philistine; George Hunter; James, Ben, Jack, and Katie Ipekjian for family warmth and good food; Laurie Taylor of Ivy Hill Interiors; Chris Wright at Jaap Romijn and Friends; Rich Pearlstein and the others at Jared Polsky & Associates; Del Martin of Jax Rugs; Bruce Johnson; the Judson Family of the Judson Stained Glass Studios; Paul Kemner and Peggy Zdila; Carl Kiss; Harvey and Ellen Knell for providing me such adequate housing during my initial researches; Larry Kreisman for introducing us to Seattle Architecture; Brian and Bonnie Krueger; Melinda Patton and John Benriter at The Lanterman House; Jodi Larusson; Robert Leary, and Rory Cunningham for introducing me to the delights of West Adams; John Lomas; Robert and Ann Luse; Sue Mack and Kevin Rodel for Irish music and pizza; Randell Makinson, not just for room and board but for encouragement, friendship, and the wisdom that comes from having been there before; Jim Marrin; Lucinda Eddy, and

Sandra Watson at The Marston House; Janice McDuffie of the Roycroft Potters; Carol Mead and Phil Baker for a night in their bungalow, and Sighly for reminding me that the study of history still can be held in one's dreams; Jerry Cohen of the Mission Oak Shop; Vance Koehler at the Moravian Tile and Pottery Works; Clay Lancaster, who has always been a source of inspiration; Jack Moore; Thomas and David Moser; Anita and Robert Munman; The New England Artisans Guild; Nancy Parsons for her warmth, friendship, and support; Ed Pinson and Debra Ware; David, Suzanne, Elaine, and Michelle of David Rago Arts and Crafts; Jim and Maxine Risley; Babs Rodieck for sharing her home to strangers knocking on her door; Paula Healy at Rose Valley; special thanks to Kitty Turgeon and Robert Rust of Roycroft for not only freely sharing information but for their supportive encouragement and good food; David Rudd of Daltons for introducing me not only to Gustav Stickley's home but to the architectural wonders of Syracuse; Lee Sanders of Black Widow fame; Kathy Carnall of the Sherwin-Williams archives; Victoria Shoemaker; Bronwyn Smith for Beaux Arts Village; all of the Audis and Brad Firkins for their courtesy when I visited L. & G. Stickley Company; Stephanie Stroup; Jim Lawrence; Alan Thomsen and Ross Fish at the Swedenborgian Church; Rick Travers, Kevin Wiens, Christ Lee, and all the guys at the Thorsen House; Joseph Taylor and Sheila Menzies of Tile Heritage; Marie Glasse Tapp of Tile Restoration Center; Raymond Tillman; Harlean Tobin; Sarah Wildasin of United Crafts; Peter van Vaulkenberg; Jerome Venneman; Joanna Fyon and Elsie Senuta at the John Wingate Weeks Memorial Home; Randell Wright; Ann Wallace; Robert Walsh; Peter and Kathy West; the ubiquitous Robert Winter; Eric Gardner at Wood Classics; George Zaffle; and last, alphabetically but never least, Debey Zito.

I would like to single out for thanks photographers with whom I have worked, all of whom not only are exceptional lensmen but, further, have a deep understanding of the movement: Tom Engler, Tom Heinz, Ed Ikuta, Ray Stubblebine, Alex Vertikoff, and James Via.

Gratitude cannot be adequately expressed to Tim Hansen and Dianne Ayres, not just for the substance and riches of their knowledge, which was invaluable; not for merely the wealth of their materials, resources that they have spent years and funds gathering into a masterful collection, materials that they trusted to us and encouraged us to use within this book; more than all this, gratitude must be expressed for their encouragement, friendship, discussions over dinner and suggestions over coffee, all of which have gone towards making this book much more than we could have accomplished by ourselves. I would also like to give a special thanks to the members of the family of Charles Greene, especially Thomas Gordon and Betty Greene, the late Ann Roberts, and Bettie Greene—for it was by research on Charles Greene that we were introduced to the beauty and import of the Arts and Crafts movement.

And then, we must give great thanks to Gail Yngve, our long-suffering editor (is there any other kind) who believed in us and this book sufficiently to encourage, persevere, push, and at times inspire us to do more than we thought ourselves capable of. And lastly, but never least, to our parents, to Sosha, and to Tamara.

INTRODUCTION

A HOUSE THAT I LOVE; with a reasonable love I think: for though my words may give you no idea of any special charm about it, yet I assure you that the charm is there; so much has the old house grown up out of the soil and the lives of those that lived on it: some thin thread of tradition, a half-anxious sense of the delight of meadow and acre and wood and river; a certain amount (not too much let us hope) of common sense, a liking for making materials serve one's turn, and perhaps at bottom some little grain of sentiment; this I think was what went to the making of the old house.

—WILLIAM MORRIS

The Arts and Crafts movement began as a movement of craft and artistic reform layered upon a desire for economic, political, and social reform. When a movement sets out to change the world, it must choose where to begin: with the large, the grandiose, the redesign of cities, the redistribution of economics, the reappraisal of the political system or with the small and inner needs—with work, with artwork and handcraftsmanship, with family and home, with ourselves. The Arts and Crafts movement, while masquerading at times as a movement concerned with the large, was in reality obsessed with the inner world, with the daily value of work in our lives, with the ability to use our hands to craft objects, with the moral quality of the design of our homes, with finding again that unity, that sense of community, that has been lost in our society. It was a movement of the individual, of reform for the individual, and of the search for and the finding of a new sense of beauty, of art, in our work, in our homes, and in our lives.

It was all of this for its duration, a too-brief period that lasted roughly from the end of the nineteenth century up to the First World War. One can find the American roots of the movement in the Philadelphia 1876 Centennial Exposition, when not only were American craftsmen introduced to the work of English designers and Japanese craftsmen who greatly influenced the future movement, but also influenced were future Arts and Crafts figures, such as Candace Wheeler, M. Louise McLaughlin, and Maria Longworth Nichols. Their courses were set by what they saw at this celebration of the nation's centenary.

Still, the true genesis of the Arts and Crafts movement was in England, not America, and primarily in the work of William Morris, the English poet, designer, and social reformer. As an undergraduate at Oxford, Morris had read and was inspired by the writings of the art critic John Ruskin, especially his

"All the stamped metals, and artificial stones, and imitation woods and bronzes, over the invention of which we hear daily exultation—all the short, and cheap, and easy ways of doing that whose difficulty is its honour—are just so many new obstacles in our already encumbered road. They will not make one of us happier or wiser— they will extend neither the pride of judgment nor the privilege of enjoyment. They will only make us shallower in our understandings, colder in our hearts, and feebler in our wits. And most justly. For we are not sent into this world to do anything into which we can not put our hearts. We have certain work to do for our bread, and that is to be done strenuously; other work to do for our delight, and that is to be done heartily; neither is to be done by halves nor shifts, but with a will; and what is not worth this effort is not to be done at all."

—JOHN RUSKIN,
THE SEVEN LAMPS OF ARCHITECTURE

influential chapter "The Nature of Gothic," in *The Stones of Venice,* which was published during Morris's time at Oxford. Ruskin, with his criticism of industrialization, his total rejection of the use of the machine, and especially his belief that society could be saved only if one could change the nature of work, lit a fire in Morris that set the direction of his life's work. Morris not only became adept at crafts, from designing wallpaper to the dyeing of cloth and the weaving of tapestries, but he preached his ideals, providing inspiration in turn for others around him and for those who followed.

Then, in London, on Friday, May 11, 1888, a group of his acolytes gathered to form an exhibition society in order to show the public their combined crafts. The motion was made that the phrase "Arts and Crafts Exhibition Society" be used to name the group. Quickly, the name came to be adopted as a designation for the movement at large. Within a decade, a number of other Arts and Crafts societies had formed. In America, an Arts and Crafts society was formed in San Francisco in 1896, a year later in Boston, Rochester, and Chicago. The first actual Arts and Crafts society in America was the Chalk and Chisel Club, established in 1895 in Minneapolis; but by 1899 it, too, had changed its name to the Minneapolis Arts and Crafts Society. The writings of Ruskin had been well read in America since the 1860s, but one found the more direct message of the Arts and Crafts movement carried across the Atlantic both by the printed word and by word of mouth. *The Studio,* the magazine that most actively promoted the work of the English Arts and Crafts movement, was read in America from its initial publication in 1893 and by 1897 was issuing an American edition called *The International Studio.* Morris never visited America, but a number of his followers did. Walter Crane lectured and exhibited his work in 1891; Charles Ashbee lectured three times, traveling across America and meeting leaders of the American movement, including Frank Lloyd Wright and Charles Greene; William Morris's daughter May Morris came in 1909 to lecture on costume and pattern design, embroidery, and jewelry.

The leaders of the American movement, in their turn, traveled to England, many of them receiving their initial inspiration from these visits. It was after Elbert Hubbard visited Morris's Kelmscott Press in 1894, possibly meeting Morris, that upon his return to America he founded his Roycroft Press, which provided both a platform for his expostulating on the movement and a base for his Roycroft empire. In 1898, Gustav Stickley traveled to an Arts and Crafts-imbued England and upon returning began his production of Craftsman furniture and started his magazine, *The Craftsman,* to spread the word of the movement. The first two issues of his magazine were dedicated respectively to William Morris and John Ruskin. Ernest Batchelder spent time working

"Men were not intended to work with the accuracy of tools, to be precise and perfect in all their actions. If you will have that precision out of them you must unhumanise them.

"If you will make a man of the working creature you cannot make a tool. Let him but begin to imagine, to think, to try to do anything worth doing, and…out come all his roughness, all his incapacity…failure after failure…but out comes the whole majesty of him also.

"We want one man to be always thinking, and another to be always working, and we call one man a gentleman, and the other an operative; whereas the workman ought often to be thinking, and the thinker often to be working, and both should be gentlemen, in the best sense… It would be well if all of us were good handicraftsmen in some kind, and the dishonour of manual labour done away with altogether. [We see] the degradation of the operative into a machine… It is not that men are ill fed, but that they have no pleasure in the work by which they make their bread and therefore look to wealth as the only means of pleasure."

—JOHN RUSKIN, *THE STONES OF VENICE*

at Charles Ashbee's Guild of Handicraft before starting his own tile-making company in California.

It is as important to understand what the Arts and Crafts movement entailed as it is to understand how it came about. It has been called an impulse, a style, an ideal, a motivation, a movement; it was all of these. One can see its manifestations in the work of craftspeople, designers, and architects; people, such as Harvey Ellis, Irving Gill, Greene and Greene, Elbert Hubbard, Bernard Maybeck, Charles Rohlfs, Gustav Stickley, Candace Wheeler, and Frank Lloyd Wright. To look at their styles, to see how drastically they varied is ample evidence that there is no one style to the movement. Yet it would not be too much to say that they were all lit within by the same burning fire, by the same idealized passion.

It was a passion to reform, to guide society back to a healthier, more simple, lifestyle; one where craft could be appreciated, not only for its artfulness but for the value its making gave to both the maker and the user. There was a new affection for nature, for the world outdoors in both the garden and the mountains, as a remedy for the cold harshness of the new industrialized world. There was a quest for home, for family, for a life where work and craft brought one closer to the people nearby rather than farther from them.

Charles A. Keeler began constructing this simple 1907 studio in the Claremont area of northern California shortly after his wife's death, as if to console his pain. The studio was and still is surrounded by mature redwood trees and a creek that meanders through the quietly secluded property. The studio itself stands rooted to the ground by the massive rocks that form the fireplace and part of the foundation.

A staircase leading up to the second floor of a 1902 Berkeley, California, chalet-style house designed by Bernard Maybeck for George Boke is made of unpainted redwood as was the rest of the home's woodwork, both structural and finish. The woodwork was left to age naturally so it acquired a warm glow over time.

SPACE

WE HAVE PLANNED HOUSES from the first that are based on the big fundamental principles of honesty, simplicity, and usefulness—the kind of houses that children will rejoice all their lives to remember as 'home,'

and that give a sense of peace and comfort to the tired men who go back to them when the day's work is done. Because we believe that the healthiest and happiest life is that which main-

A watercolor drawing by Harvey Ellis, published in the October 1905 issue of The Craftsman *magazine, showing the use of built-in benches that define spaces by function but do not totally separate them.*

tains the closest relationship with out-of-doors, we have planned our houses with outdoor living rooms, dining rooms, and sleeping rooms and many windows to let in plenty of air and sunlight.

—GUSTAV STICKLEY, *CRAFTSMAN HOMES*

Home space. It is the space where people dance, sit, read, sleep, share meals with family and friends, laugh, feel secure, face the world. The idea of space changed drastically with houses built under the influence of the Arts and Crafts movement. Interiors opened up, floor plans became more asymmetrical, the uses of space became more flexible, small spaces assumed new meanings, life within the house flowed more freely, and there was a strong bonding made between space within the home and with the natural world outside.

The tendency in the traditional American family home had been to segregate activities—the kitchen and pantry set off from the main body of the house, sometimes in separate quarters, the parlor kept pristine for visitors, the sitting room set aside for the family to gather in the evening. Then as the nineteenth century drew to a close and the next century

Rooms flow one into another in this Berkeley, California, house.

began, life became more informal; the idea of the designed home shifted downward from being an upper-class right to becoming a right of the upper-middle and aspiring working class. Since schooling was now done outside the home, the home grew smaller; meals became more relaxed and had fewer courses; entrance halls became luxuries rather than social necessities; working-class girls worked less often as servants and more often in factories. Between 1900 and 1920 the number of domestic servants in America declined by half, from eighty to thirty-nine per thousand.

With the change from post-and-beam construction to the innovation of the balloon frame as well as the technological advancement of factory production of nails and standardized mill cutting of lumber, not only did it become cheaper and faster to build homes, it opened up the possibilities for interior space, both figuratively and literally. Before the advent of the balloon frame, interior space was limited to the distance a beam could be safely stretched between two posts. After balloon-frame construction began in about 1840, the house could be raised in wall sections, each supporting the other in a lightweight frame that left the interior space opened up to a new sense of freedom.

This fireplace is in the front hall at the Duncan Irwin House in Pasadena, California. Note the roughness of the clinker brick often favored by Greene and Greene.

THE FIREPLACE

It is enough to say that in these days a home can scarcely be considered worthy of the name if it does not contain at least one hearth. Some inexplicable quality of wood fires exerts almost a hypnotic influence upon those who eagerly gather about them. The smoldering glow of the logs induces a calm and introspective mood that banishes all the trivialities and distractions of the day's work and gives one an opportunity to replenish his store of energy for the coming day.

—HENRY SAYLOR

The fireplace and the hearth were, for those of the Arts and Crafts movement, the heart, the center, the soul of the house. Around it, the house was built; around it, the life of the family evolved. Henry Saylor, in writing about the fireplace, told of the man who defined the home as "a fireplace, boxed in." No more was it needed for heat—since the cast-iron radiator had been put into mass production in the last decade of the century, central heating had filled the need of keeping the middle-class family warm during the winter. Rather than eliminating the need for the fireplace, central heating allowed architects and builders to place the fireplace in sometimes less-than-functional locations and to use the fireplace for

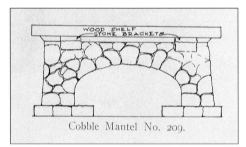

Cobble Mantel No. 209.

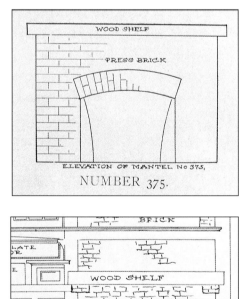

ELEVATION OF MANTEL No 375.

NUMBER 375.

A fireplace found in the boys' bedroom at the Gamble House. Although designed by the Greenes, this fireplace is more conventional in style and execution except for the detail ornament above the mantelpiece.

These are typical turn-of-the-century fireplaces built for middle-class American homes. A wide variety of mantels could be chosen from catalogs, especially for mail-order bungalows. (From the Bungalow Book, *by Henry H. Wilson.)*

a role other than that of heating. Frank Lloyd Wright, for example, did not hesitate to place a fireplace in a large open space dividing two rooms, where it could not effectively heat either side; but that was not the point of the fireplace for Wright. Its purpose was to fulfill a more metaphorical role. As the house itself came to be spoken of in almost anthropomorphic terms, the fireplace, the hearth, took on the role of the beating heart. "A home without at least one fireplace," *House and Garden* reported in 1909, "can hardly be considered livable." Saylor, again about the fireplace, wrote, "A bungalow without a fireplace would be almost as much of an anomaly as a garden without flowers—and as cheerless."

THE INGLENOOK

The inglenook forms a place for retreat, for privacy and intimacy—never opening directly to the outside, never fully closed off from the inside of the house. It serves, in a sense, as the innermost depth of the public part of the house. In a further sense, it provides a way for the heart of the home, the fireplace, to be protected, to form a space in which one can turn inward, to contemplate the firelight, to share times with someone special.

Oddly, the advent of popularity of this innermost space of the house happened as the inside of the house was opening up, was moving away from the Victorian sense of closed, tightly defined spaces and moving towards the more modern sense of openness and flexibility of space.

The use of inglenooks in the home was an innovation revived by the English architects Richard Norman Shaw and Eden Nesfield in the mid-1860s. They adapted to the upper-middle-class home an element of traditional farmhouse architecture that dates back to the late fifteenth century: the hearth (the ingle), situated in its own alcove (the nook.) In America, the inglenook was established in the 1880s by the work of H. H. Richardson as part of the new American architectural vocabulary.

Hermann Muthesius in his 1896 study of the English home, *Das Englische Haus,* wrote that the inglenook was

"…the old form of domestic hearth as it existed in English farmhouses in the room in which the cooking was done and the family lived; and in as much as one derives most benefit from the warmth of the fire by sitting close to it, it is the exact equivalent of the old German tiled stove surrounded by stone seats." He noted that it was "…important that the seats should have direct light to enable people to sit and read there. An outside wall is therefore the only possible place for an inglenook, which is seen as a jutting extension, a very familiar motif in the external appearance of the English house. Inside, the alcove is always just high enough for a person to stand upright in it."

Above: This inglenook is a mixture of English and Craftsman styles, the design first published in Craftsman Home.

This is a Japonisme-style inglenook, first shown in American Homes and Gardens, *1912.*

In bungalows and early twentieth-century homes, there were no clear distinctions made between a living room and a dining room. The carpet is currently made by JAX rugs.

INTERIOR SPACE

During the time of the Arts and Crafts movement, the division in the interior spaces of the home became, at times, more visual than actual—a screen placed within a room could isolate a private corner; a built-in half-bookcase could divide a large room into two; two benches could form an alcove. The more private parts of the home—the bedrooms, the bathrooms,—retained their traditional distinct divisions, but in the more public parts of the home—the library, the living room, the den, the dining room—unity was achieved both by creating the openness of flow within the space as well by developing an accord in the interior design elements.

The opening up of the interior and the change in the uses of the space reflected both the desired and actual changes that were taking place in society. From the time of the Queen Anne movement in architecture, the house had exploded outward with porches, sleeping porches, pergolas, and trellises. On the inside, the formal parlor was transformed into the more used, informal living room. Gradually, as space became more open, the dining room opened into the living room and library, and the house opened up into the outdoors.

THE FIRST CRAFTSMAN HOUSE: MR. STICKLEY'S SYRACUSE HOME

The February 1903 issue of *The Craftsman* magazine included an article about the newly remodeled Syracuse home of its publisher and editor, Gustav Stickley. On Christmas Eve of the year before, his house had been gutted by a fire, prompting him to completely redesign his home's interior and furnishings.

It was a pivotal time in the career of this young entrepreneur. Stickley had been producing his Mission-style Craftsman furniture only for four years, and he was just a few months short of the time that he would be publishing and promoting his Craftsman house designs

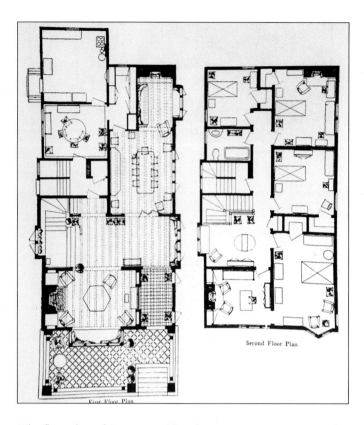

The floor plan of Gustav Stickley's home in Syracuse, New York.

under the influence of the great designer and architect Harvey Ellis.

Stickley's home, built in 1900, was an unremarkable neocolonial on the exterior. Remodeled after the fire, it has a quite remarkable openness of interior for the time, an openness that retained an amazing degree of privacy for Mr. Stickley and his family. In the plans of the first floor, a person sitting next to the fireplace in the living room can look through the living room, through the open front hall, through the dining room, all the way to the library at the back of the house, a stretch of some sixty-six feet. In the reverse, one seated in the library can see the flickering of the fireplace at the front of the house. Yet, coming into the house, a visitor can barely see the dining room or library because of a folding screen that blocks the view, and a person must make two left turns in order to enter the living room.

Stickley's biographer, Mary Ann Smith, has pointed out how much the interior of the home resembles his Craftsman furniture. *The Craftsman* article quotes a visitor asking Stickley, "Have you no ornament, carving or draperies in your house, Mr. Stickley?"

In Gustav Stickley's Syracuse, New York, house, a visitor can see the elements that give unity to the openness of the interior space—the parallel ceiling beams left exposed, the paneling on the walls, the wood flooring that runs uninterrupted from room to room.

"No draperies, thank you, and as for ornament— have we not our friends?"

As Smith points out, unity is created in the separate elements of the interior by two key elements. First, the horizontal band running at the tops of the doors and windows connects all the walls on the ground floor. Below this band, the "walls are paneled with vertical boards; above, they are plastered." Then secondly, the squared rectangular beams that run the length of the house, from the living room to the library, emphasize the perspective openness of the interior space. As the floor of broad chestnut boards spreads continuously throughout the downstairs space, the only division between rooms becomes the cross beams that serve as a visual separation.

EXTERIOR SPACES

There was a craze for sleeping porches at the turn of the century. As a writer for *The Ladies' Home Journal* wrote in 1910, "In these days when fresh air and sunshine are considered so essential to good health, no home is complete without a sleeping-porch." Fueled by a newfound concern for healthy living, there was a belief that porch-life meant that incipient lung trouble could be cured and one could live longer and be healthier. Some enthusiastic writers even advocated their readers to sleep outdoors when the thermometer was at zero.

There were many styles of sleeping porches. One kind, open throughout the year, was especially popular in the warm climate of southern California. Others were enclosed or half enclosed with glass doors and windows. Some were used for dining rooms, living rooms, and nursery rooms. Stylistically, too, there emerged variegated forms. Archetypical was the elegant wooden porch with overhanging roof that was well suited to the moderate climate of California and was typical of those designed by the Greene brothers. On the other end of the spectrum was the unique and inexpensive kind that used only a sheet of denim to cover the roof. It cost only three to ten dollars and looked more like a tent, but in its spirit was the distant cousin of the elegant porches designed by the Greenes.

As porches, sleeping porches, piazzas, and terraces created new outdoor living spaces, furniture suitable for outdoors became necessary accouterments to make them livable—places to rest and entertain. There were three main styles of outdoor furniture often cited in period magazines. One was the simple, painted, geometric wooden furniture. Often painted white, it was clearly influenced by then-popular German/Austrian style, characterized by its straight lines. Another was unpainted hickory furniture made of rustic, crooked branches of hickory. The last and most popular of the three was woven furniture made of willow, rattan, or native grass.

Woven furniture was not, in itself, particularly identified with the Arts and Crafts movement, but between 1890 and 1920, many pieces designed in styles associated with the movement were manufactured. Beyond the tons of rattan furniture imported from China, Americans began producing pieces during the Victorian period that were ornate with spiral patterns and curvilinear legs. Then, from the 1890s onward, appealing to the change in taste, they flooded the market with a simpler, more geometric style of woven furniture. In 1893, Joseph McHugh of the Popular Shop in New York, who was just

Top: These three illustrations of sleeping porches from The Ladies' Home Journal *were of the least expensive kinds, made of canvas, denim, or tent fabric.*

Bottom: Almost every room in the Duncan Irwin House opens up to this central courtyard with a square lily pond in the middle. The house is located in the corner lot, exposed to the traffic and is an example of one way to create an indoor/outdoor space while retaining a high level of privacy.

Courtyard of the Duncan Irwin House.

a few years hence to introduce his line of "Mission furniture," introduced a line of wicker furniture, "McHugh willow." A shrewd businessman, his furniture was designed and constructed in a simple manner that proved to be immensely popular. It was not until 1907 that Gustav Stickley introduced his Craftsman Willow Furniture line, modeled after Austrian and German wicker styles. By 1908, wicker furniture became so popular in America that more than 160 manufacturers were in operation. The kinds of woven furniture ranged so widely that one could find an easy chair with arms, a dining-room set, a lamp shade with stands, a candleholder, a swing, a wooden basket covered with wicker, a tea cart, a tea tray, and an umbrella stand, all on a pleasant sunny porch.

The colors that were popular for the porch furniture were either those of Craftsman hues, such as forest green, nut brown, Delft blue, ebony, sealing-wax red, Spanish yellow, indigo blue, or emerald green on the stained wicker, or the pastel colors for those who painted their wooden furniture in the 1910s. These pieces became popular not only because they went aesthetically well with the then-popular Mission-style furniture, but also because they added the feeling of a mountain resort in suburban homes during the time when people were seeking relief from the turmoils of life in a city.

In southern California, the climate is so temperate and the belief of the health benefits of sleeping in the open air so pervasive that the sleeping porch defines a new way of life. On this porch of the Pasadena Gamble House, the two Gamble boys slept overlooking the Arroyo Seco not only in the hot summer months but throughout the year.

A present-day version of Craftsman-style home, drawn by George Hunter, a northern California artist and artisan.

INDOORS AND OUTDOORS

The April 1906 issue of *The Craftsman* featured "A Convenient Bungalow with Separate Kitchen and Open-air Dining Room," which was described as a house "reduced to its simplest form, where life may be carried on with the greatest amount of freedom and comfort and the least amount of effort." This bungalow had a deeply recessed front porch, "which is meant to be used as a small outdoor sitting room," and then, a unique feature, an open porch that connected the separate kitchen to the main part of the house, creating a space that "is intended for an outdoor dining room that shall be sufficiently sheltered from storms to allow the outdoor life to go on through any sort of weather." Though intended as a summer cottage, and certainly not typical, this bungalow more than amply expressed the desire of the period to bring the outdoors within and allow the indoors to stretch outside. Most bungalows were not this dramatic, but the majority would bring the out-of-doors inside through the use of large windows, opening up to grass and trees, or through enclosed entry verandahs, serving as midway rooms between the interior and the exterior. Then the

Hickory furniture and woven furniture were used both indoors and outdoors. Advertisement for the Rustic Hickory Furniture in American Homes and Gardens, *1912.*

natural world was often implied within the home by the motifs chosen for the stencils and curtain embroidery, or in the colors of paint used, or even by the actual bark being left upon a supporting beam within an interior. One can find this sort of reference to the outdoors being used in the rusticity of the log cabin that Gustav Stickley built at Craftsman Farms or in the roughness of the board-and-batten interiors and cobblestone fireplaces so popular on the West Coast.

The Arturo Bandini House, built around a sunny courtyard.

THE BANDINI HOME

In 1903, Arturo Bandini of an old respected California family requested the brothers Charles and Henry Greene to build a "California house" for him. The brothers built a house, possibly modeled upon something they had read in the popular novel of the period, *Ramona*—a simple U-shaped structure of redwood board-and-batten built around a central garden with all the rooms opening onto the courtyard. As described by Randell Makinson, a verandah formed a space between "the sheltered and cave-like atmosphere" inside and the courtyard garden outside. Life was meant to be lived in both spaces, was meant to flow between the inside and the outside. The courtyard, in a sense, actually provided an additional

The Bandini House, built in 1903 for Arturo Bandini by Greene and Greene, was based on the U-shaped pattern, which corresponded to the California Mission-style courtyard.

living space for the Bandini family, three sides of it being protected by the enclosure of the house, the fourth side having the effect of being walled in by the freestanding pergola and the end of the garden.

The outdoors were further expressed by the two massive fireplaces made from cobblestones from the nearby Arroyo that provided warmth to the living and dining rooms. In the hearth of the living-room fireplace, Mr. Bandini had placed two large, flat handmade bricks, which were from the old San Fernando Mission. As Charles Greene wrote of this house, "It is all of wood and very simple"—a house ideally suited to the freedom of life between the indoors and outdoors that the Californian climate encouraged.

From its first publication in 1884, the best-selling novel Ramona, *by Helen Hunt Jackson, about life in a Southern California Mission courtyard, fascinated Americans with a romanticized image of the Spanish past. The mythology of Ramona spread, and the fictitious site of Ramona's marriage was given an actual location in San Diego that attracted many tourists.*

One can see the possible influence upon the Greenes from the best-selling novel *Ramona,* which they had read when they first came out to California in 1893. The California home of Ramona, a typical house of the Mexican period of California, is described:

The house was of adobe, low, with a wide verandah on the three sides of the inner court, and a still broader one across the entire front, which looked to the south. These verandahs, especially those on the inner court, were supplementary rooms to the house. The greater part of the family life went on in them. Nobody stayed inside the walls, except when it was necessary. All the kitchen work, except the actual cooking, was done here, in front of the kitchen doors and windows. Babies slept, were washed, sat in the dirt, and played on the verandah. The women said their prayers, took their naps, and wove their lace there…The herdsmen and shepherds smoked there, lounged there, trained their dogs there; there the young made love, and the old dozed; the benches, which ran the entire length of the walls, were worn into hollows, and shone like satin; the tiled floors also were broken and sunk in places, making little wells, which filled up in times of hard rains, and were then an invaluable addition to the children's resources for amusement, and also to the comfort of the dogs, cats, and fowls, who picked about them, taking sips from each.

THE EAST COAST

THE ARTS AND CRAFTS movement in the eastern United States, more than elsewhere in the nation, strove towards finding a balance between the need to pay homage to its English heritage and, from the turn of the century, the almost effervescent bursting forth of that independent democratic spirit that was so uniquely American. More than any other one event, the Arts and Crafts exhibitors at the 1901 Pan-American Exposition in Buffalo, New York, marked the transformation.

The masses came to the Exposition to see the "Rainbow City"; they came to have fun at the

East Coast architecture of the Arts and Crafts movement was richly influenced by the movement in England. Looking through the hallway into the living room of this house in Plymouth, Massachusetts, one can see how the interior is more rigid in terms of its floor plans in contrast to the open flow of the inside of a California bungalow. Originally built in 1910 and meticulously restored by David E. Berman in 1995, today it is open to the public as a bed and breakfast.

honky-tonk amusements of the midway and to see the Electric Tower, the 375-foot-high, lighted testimonial to the fact that the age of steam was over and the electric age was upon them. The fair was a statement that this was a new century with a new world order. The vision for that new order could be perceived by restricting the exhibition to work accomplished in the Western Hemisphere, eliminating all possible competition from Europe.

The central courtyard in the Manufacturers and Liberal Arts Building, where many products of the new progressive industrialism were on display, was originally set out to be a garden; but under pressure from the National Arts Club of New York City, the fair administrators allowed it to become metamorphosed into an "Art Court," a place of display for the newly burgeoning Arts and Crafts movement in America. Louis Comfort Tiffany of the National Arts Club supplied the design that enclosed the courtyard under four plain glass domes and arranged exhibitors around the perimeter, and, as a centerpiece, placed a grand fountain of colored favrile glass. Strategically located in a corner, Gustav Stickley's United Craftsman Company was showing for the first time to the general public his new line of Craftsman furniture. He shared space with the Grueby Faience Company out of Boston, which had been producing a line of art wares for about four years. The Rookwood Pottery from Cincinnati was also there and, along with Grueby and Tiffany, was awarded a gold medal. The National Arts Club entry brought pottery by Newcombe Pottery, Charles Volkmar, and Adelaide Alsop Robineau into the courtyard. Charles Rohlfs, a local furniture maker, not only had an exhibit of his Gothic-styled furniture but also furnished the displays of several manufacturers of other products with his work. Gorham Manufacturing Company, an old Rhode Island firm, was also there exhibiting their new Martelé line of silver work, a line that demonstrated the recent fashionable innovation of leaving the hammer marks of the craftsman on the works to proclaim the handmade nature of the product.

All of this signaled change—change in the way the applied arts were being classified, change in the degree of dependence upon British names, and most of all, change in the very character of the work being produced. In the work of Stickley and others, one could see a move away from the ornate medievalism and naturalism of the English movement and a move towards simplicity, towards an emphasis upon overly visible craftsmanship. This change was probably most directly signaled by the introduction at the Exposition of the new line of furniture by Joseph P. McHugh & Company that introduced the new word *mission* into the movement. McHugh's New York City store, The Popular Shop, had been open since shortly after the 1876 Centennial Exposition in Philadelphia and, by the turn of the century after carefully gauging changes in fashion through the years, was marketing the products of Liberty's of London, chintzes by William Morris, and wallpaper by Walter Crane, along with the still-popular imitation, New England furniture of the eighteenth and nineteenth centuries. He used the 1901 Buffalo Exposition to expose the public to his Mission style by furnishing the reception room of the New York State Building with forty-eight pieces of it. Though not a standard exhibit, it was still awarded a silver medal.

Even though it was Tiffany who had modeled his company upon the English example set by Morris and Company, the company that arranged for the existence of the "Art Court" for artisans, the goods on display in Buffalo were for the first time a blazon proclamation of

The "Briar Rose" wallpaper by Bradbury and Bradbury is the backdrop for a detail of a chair built by David Berman, using a design of the English Arts and Crafts architect C. F. A. Voysey.

In this original view of the exterior of the log house at Craftsman Farms in Morris Plains, New Jersey, note the massive chimney and fireplace made of rubble stone. The first story of the home displays the natural log exterior; the second story is shingled.

the move towards that which was uniquely American. It was a move away from the influence of the English Arts and Crafts movement and a move toward the simple, a simplicity that verged upon rusticity. It was also a move towards the mass marketing at which Americans have excelled.

GUSTAV STICKLEY AND HIS CRAFTSMAN FARMS

One autumn evening in 1912, standing in a woodland-bordered pasture and looking down over the Craftsman Farms, Gustav Stickley told a visitor, "This is my Garden of Eden. This is the realization of the dreams that I had when I worked as a lad." His work as a lad had been the hard work of a stonemason's tender for his German emigrant father. "It was heavy and tedious labor," he wrote, "much too hard for a boy of my age, and being put to it so early gave me an intense dislike for it." But it was the kind of work that can put yearnings and hungers into a young man's heart, that can drive him towards recognition and success, and that can give him the strength and energy to achieve long-held dreams.

The Craftsman Farms were the realization of one of these long-held dreams for Gustav Stickley. His father had deserted the family while Gustav was still in his teens, so he went to work in his uncle's furniture factory to help support the large family. By the time he was twenty-six, he had opened a furniture store with one of his brothers, and within two years he had begun the manufacture of furniture.

By 1898, as he turned forty, he had been involved in a number of furniture-manufacturing operations, but, in the words of his biographer Mary Ann Smith, "...there seems to have been a restlessness in his life." That year he traveled to England. Exactly where he visited and who he saw in England is not known. Morris had been dead for two years, and Ruskin was mentally incapacitated; but according to John Crosby Freeman's early biographical history of Stickley, he did meet T. J. Cobden-Sanderson, William Lethaby, Charles Ashbee, and C. F. A. Voysey. Smith hypothesizes that he might have seen the Green Dining Room in the South Kensington Museum, the complete interior executed by William Morris and Company, or he possibly might have seen examples of the work of the English Arts and Crafts movement by visiting the actual premises of Morris and Company or Ashbee's Guild of Handicraft retail shop, or Liberty and Company on Regent Street.

A contemporary view of the Craftsman Farmhouse dining room.

Upon his return to America, Stickley started his own furniture manufacturing operation and, in his own words, "…stopped using the standard patterns and finishes, and began to make all kinds of furniture after my own designs, independently of what other people were doing, or of any necessity to fit my designs, woods, and finishes to any other factory." His new designs were exhibited for the first time at the furniture trade show in Grand Rapids in July of 1900, and by year's end he had leased a building in a fashionable area of downtown Syracuse, New York, for his operations, now named United Crafts and modeled on a medieval guild system, with a profit-sharing system for his employees. In 1901, he began the magazine, *The Craftsman,* and by 1904, when he had written the first early history of his operations, *What is Wrought in the Craftsman Workshops,* he had, if the history is accurate, over two hundred workers in his growing empire—needleworkers sewing pillows, table runners, and lamp shades; metalworkers hammering not just furniture hardware but the trays, vases, and lighting fixtures that he was now marketing. He had an area set aside just for making the rush seats for his chairs and another area set aside for the leather workers. He had also adopted the motto *Als Ik Kan,* roughly meaning "As I Can," that was described in the 1904 history as "the condensed expression of a great energy, which neither fears disaster nor knows defeat."

His accomplishments, though, were the results of more than just a great energy; vision was there—a dream formed and held. Part of his vision was for a community of like-minded people. In 1904, he traveled west by train, visiting Arizona and California. Stopping for a visit in Palm Springs, he stayed the evening in a tent cottage of a hotel, where his "…thoughts reverted to a scheme long cherished in my fancy, but for which I had vainly tried to find a suitable place of execution."

In an article he wrote later for *The Craftsman,* Stickley outlined a scheme for a community of craftspeople: "…each worker could make whatever he desired in his own home or workshop.… A board of managers might be chosen to examine articles intended for sale, which after being successfully subjected to a thorough examination, should be stamped with the community seal, as a final absolute mark of approval. All foodstuffs, with the exception of a few luxuries, could be produced in the region, and each family could own a producing area large enough to supply its wants." The community was not unlike Ashbee's Guild of Handicraft, which was in operation in England during his visit, having just recently relocated

The original dining room at the Craftsman Farmhouse was sufficiently lit by diamond-shaped windows on three sides of the room while the portiere was hung on the fourth side that led into the adjoining living room. The massive logs of the walls and ceiling are chestnut and finished with a wood oil that gives a delightful sunny tone. Half hidden by these logs, the ceiling flat boards are constructed of hemlock, stained light olive green.

The log house at Craftsman Farms as it appears today.

out into the countryside at Chipping Campden, and not unlike the communities begun at Rose Valley outside Philadelphia and the Woodstock, New York, community of Byrdcliffe. However, Stickley's dreams for a community in California never materialized.

Then, in June of 1908, Stickley purchased land and wrote, "I am preparing to establish a school for the definite working out of the theory I have so long held of reviving practical and profitable handicrafts in connection with small farming carried on my modern methods of intensive agriculture." The land he bought had "… heavily wooded hills, little wandering brooks, low-lying meadows, and plenty of garden and orchard land," and he started making plans for the building of his home. "For the first time I am applying to my own house, and working out in practical detail, all the theories which so far I have applied on to the houses of other people." Here he states the golden rules of Craftsman building: first, the

house "…should be suited exactly to the requirements of the life to be lived in it; second, that it should harmonize with its environment; and third, that it should be built, so far as possible, from the materials to be had right there on the ground and left as nearly as was practicable in the natural state." In an article he wrote for *The Craftsman* magazine in 1908, he provided not just a complete description of the house as he was going to build it, but drawings of the interior and exterior elevations and complete room plans of the house of his dreams. His vision for the house was complete, even down to what he called "…the mellow coloring that prevails throughout the house," resulting from the extensive use of wood and how "… by the glow of color and the friendliness of the soft, dull surface of the wood,…a room finished in this way seems to be always filled with a mellow autumnal light, irrespective of the degree of light outside." This house, though, was not built. Another article was written

The ceiling of the Craftsman Farmhouse main room uses twenty-three logs as beams, each seven to eight inches in diameter. The stone fireplace, now unfortunately painted white, has a copper hood bearing the motto "The lyf so short, the craft so long to lerne." The lanterns that are hanging from chains were manufactured by Stickley.

for *The Craftsman* two months later describing a "Club House" that was to be built at Craftsman Farms. Plans, drawings of the interiors and the exterior, and a complete description of the "log house" were provided. This club house would be open to all the workers, students, and guests at Craftsman Farms and also to invited guests of the place. "We intend to make it a sort of central gathering place where it is hoped that many a pleasant entertainment will be held."

In 1909, Stickley bought land along Route 10, then known as the old turnpike from Newark to Mount Pleasant, about three-quarters of a mile northwest of his first parcels, where, finally, he was to build his long-

A detail of the copper hood of the main room fireplace in the Craftsman Farmhouse.

A current view of the Craftsman Farmhouse.

planned-for community. In the late summer or fall, he began construction of several bungalows, one of which he moved into at completion in the spring of 1910.

Two *Craftsman* articles appeared in August of 1910, and then in January of 1911 a visitor, called "the Traveler," came to the farm and talked with Stickley, called "the Host," discussing in broad terms the vision that the Host had for a Farm-school. He quotes the Host as saying (in a paraphrase of John Ruskin), "I believe that the workman should have as much diversity of manual instruction and practice as the man who relies on his brain must have in his intellectual pursuits, and that one should supplement the other; that is, the laborer must use his brain and soul and use them well; the brain-worker must cultivate both interest and practical experience in manual endeavor." Later that same day, the Traveler "drew his chair to the great hearth where the logs cut in the afternoon were blazing brightly," and questioned the Host further about his plans. The Host explains:

> The idea of the Farm-school? It is briefly this:
> A reversal of the accepted education order,
> which prescribes books first in importance.
> Only when educated, does the boy learn to

work. I believe that boys should first be taught the ideal and the practice of *doing something useful* with brain and hands, combined with abundant outdoor life. Through work the child would learn the necessity for knowledge. Study should be the valued supplement to work, and book-education should accompany, but never precede the education derived from actual individual experience.

This article becomes more specific, stating that its aim was to take "boys at the completion of the usual grammar-school period and to give them a practical education on the Farms during the years between fourteen and twenty." The boys will learn to understand the "weather and the seasons, the relation of plant life to the elements;…will learn to understand animal life and the healing properties of herbs; will learn to understand tools and how to build anything…from a chicken-coop to a house." But there is no date set for it to begin. He concludes with a description that could have been easily applied to himself:

> A mind crushed by the dull detail of routine labor
> and a physique depleted by unwholesome

indoor occupation cannot lift a man out of the narrow sphere of drudgery. But a mind lit by the vision of a larger purpose in daily work and of something greater beyond that, a body vibrant with health and ready for action,— these make a man, while loyal to his work, at the same time independent of it, because his thought and his capability are larger than the routine of his occupation.

His vision came closer to a reality in 1912 as he turned to Raymond Riordon, the founder of Interlaken, a progressive school in Michigan, to help him get it started. In an article by Riordon in the November issue of *The*

The main room is separated from the porch by only an unglazed opening. The porch, which runs the length of the building, serves as a halfway space between the outdoors and the warmth of the inside.

Craftsman that year, the specifics are given on a School for Citizenship to be opened in June of 1913 for fifty boys, age nine years and over. "They will live in craftsman houses, which they have helped to build, and each house will be a real *home* for the boys who have had the joy of helping to create it."

The construction of the Log House at Craftsman Farms had been finished by the spring or summer of 1911, and by the end of 1912, as the Riordon article was being printed, the chicken houses and cow stables were built and the horse stable was under construction. Then in May of 1913, he leased a twelve-story building in New York City across the street from Bonwit Teller and close to stores such as Tiffany's and Lord and Taylor. Except for the furniture manufacturing, he brought all the elements of his now extensive business empire under one roof. The first two floors displayed his furniture; the third and fourth floors housed his rugs, draperies, interior decorating and house furnishings showrooms. He had four floors devoted to a "Craftsman Permanent Homebuilders' Exposition." One floor was for *The Craftsman* magazine with the allied architectural and service department, another floor for the workshops to demonstrate the various crafts. The eleventh floor was for a library, lecture hall, and club rooms; and at the top of the building was a restaurant with a Grueby tiled fireplace where customers could dine on the healthful produce, eggs, and beef sent in from the Craftsman Farms.

The energy he poured into his new headquarters evidently left little time for his aspirations for the farm. In an article in the October 1913 issue of *The Craftsman* about the "Craftsman Farms, Its Development and Future," there is no mention of the school. Instead, he has reverted to a vague concept of community with no mention of craftsmen working together. The article is replete with bucolic descriptions of the farm; photographs of the cottages and the Club House are pictured as well as a photograph of "Mr. Stickley and his first granddaughter, Barbara Wiles, taken on the hillside between the Club House and one of the twin cottages."

Less than two years later, under the heading of "Business Troubles," *The New York Times* made the announcement that "petition of bankruptcy has been

Gustav Stickley with his granddaughter, Barbara Wiles, at Craftsman Farms.

filed against Gustav Stickley, the Craftsman, Inc." Stickley would eventually settle with his creditors for one-third of what he owed them. He continued to publish *The Craftsman* for another year, after which it merged with *Art World.* By August of 1917, the farms were sold and Stickley had moved with his family back to Syracuse.

ROYCROFT

Twelve Things for Roycrofters to Remember: the Value of Time, the Success of Perseverance, the Pleasure of Working, the Dignity of Simplicity, the Worth of Character, the Power of Kindness, the Influence of Example, the Obligation of Duty, the Wisdom of Economy, the Virtue of Patience, the Improvement of Talent, the Joy of Originating.
—THE PHILOSOPHY OF ELBERT HUBBARD

Elbert Hubbard tragically died one year short of his sixtieth birthday when the ship he boarded for crossing the Atlantic to Europe, the *Lusitania,* was sunk by torpedoes from a German submarine. Eight years previous, in a small book he had written and published, called *White Hyacinths,* he said that "…besides writing and public speaking, I have something to do with a semicommunistic corporation called The Roycrofters, employing upwards of five hundred people. The work of the Roycrofters is divided into departments as follows: a farm, bank, hotel, printing plant, bookbindery, furniture factory, and black-

smith shop." His "something to do with The Roycrofters" was to conceive of, organize, expand, and direct an empire that published one of the leading small magazines of the country with a circulation of over a hundred thousand.

The empire also operated an inn; manufactured furniture, copper goods, leather items, pottery, jewelry, lighting; and ran a large mail-order business that sold most of the items made at the Roycroft Campus in East Aurora, New York. In addition, he found time to write books, to write the monthly issues of his magazine, *The Philistine,* to write a monthly *Little Journey* to the homes of the famous, to lecture extensively, to pen mottoes, and to go horseback riding several times a week.

Before he began Roycroft, he had already reached a certain financial success in a partnership with his brother-in-law in the Larkin Soap Manufactory in Buffalo, New York. In the years Hubbard spent with the company, it had risen to national prominence, largely because of his genius for marketing, advertising, and promotion, but this financial success was not sufficient for his life's work. He sold out his interest in the company, took classes at Harvard, and turned to living the life of a writer. The summer of 1894 he went to England where he was introduced to the then-flourishing Arts and Crafts movement, and, inspired by a visit to William Morris's Kelmscott Press, he began a new life as a publisher and writer upon his return to America.

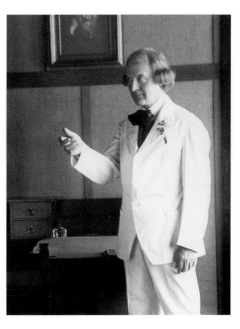

Elbert Hubbard (1856–1915)

This stained-glass window, designed by Dard Hunter, is at the Roycroft Inn.

By December of that year, his first *Little Journeys* was being printed, and in June of the year following, the first issue of *The Philistine: A Periodical of Protest* was published by his Roycroft Press; the name "Roycroft" was taken from the seventeenth-century bookbinding partners Samuel and Thomas Roycroft. Shortly thereafter, he published the first of many Roycroft books, *The Song of Songs.* His publishing necessitated a bindery, which then spawned a leather shop.

By 1896, Hubbard's little craft community was making furniture for its own use and in 1901 began offering it for sale through its mail-order catalogs. The furniture needed hardware that called for a blacksmith shop; the blacksmith shop, in turn, sired a copper shop that produced some of the finest of the Roycroft work, everything from jewelry, vases, candlesticks, and bookends to door hinges, lamps, and fireplace hoods. The Roycroft Campus, as Hubbard called his crafts community, became a nationally known tourist attraction, and, to handle the ever-increasing numbers of visitors, Hubbard enlarged what had been the original print shop and opened it as the Roycroft Inn in 1903. Honeymooners visiting the not-distant Niagara Falls would come for a day or two at Roycroft Inn; readers of *The Philistine* would often stay for a week.

The Roycroft Campus Shops operate today out of the building built by Elbert Hubbard, about 1902, to be used first for the blacksmith shop and very shortly thereafter as the Roycroft Copper Shop.

The home of Alexis Jean Fournier (1865–1948), the "court painter of the Roycroft," built after Hubbard gave him land next to the Roycroft Campus as an inducement to come to East Aurora as the artist-in-residence.

My Garden at Evening, by Alexis Jean Fournier, was painted in Fournier's backyard. The back of the Roycroft furniture shop can be seen through the trees. From the collection of Kitty Turgeon and Robert Rust.

The East Aurora, New York, Roycroft Inn had originally been the Roycroft Print Shop and was converted in 1903 to an establishment providing both room and board for the growing numbers who came to visit the Roycroft Community.

After Hubbard's death, his son Elbert (Bert) Hubbard II took over the Roycroft enterprises; but, as with many of the undertakings of the Arts and Crafts movement, it had difficulty adjusting to the different economic times, and sales rapidly declined. The copper shop closed in 1933, and the print shop, which began Roycroft, was the last shop to close in 1938. Bert Hubbard sold the inn and the buildings of the campus in May of 1939, and the inn continued operating until the 1980s when it, too, closed.

With the revival of the Arts and Crafts movement, the Roycroft Campus has come alive again. In 1996, the Roycroft Inn opened; the Roycroft Pottery has been

Guests entering the Roycroft Inn are greeted by the motto "Produce great people—the rest follows."

active for a number of years; the nonprofit Foundation for the Study of the Arts and Crafts Movement at Roycroft publishes a national newsletter and holds conferences, tours, and symposiums. Another nonprofit group, the Roycrofters-at-Large, is designating current-day craftspeople who may use a new Roycroft mark as a sign of excellence and work in the spirit of the original movement.

Lit by reproductions of the original Dard Hunter lighting fixtures, the reception room of the restored Roycroft Inn is the oldest portion of the inn, built originally as the print shop of the Roycrofters in 1897.

The Roycroft Campus today.

SURFACE

This dining room is decorated with a checkerberry pattern, adapted from Gustav Stickley's Craftsman Workshop's design for wall stencils and table runners.

ALL ARTS are alike in that the common end and aim of each is the weaving of a pattern. The pattern to be woven in the designing of a house is one of forms, lines, colors, and textures; relating, repeating, and contrasting one with the other, creating rhythms, directions, and accents. Without these rhythms and accents, without the pattern, the work remains mere building. Style is the relation of these rhythms and accents, one to the other, to create a pattern; the relation of form to form, color to color, texture to texture, and each to all creating one definite expression.

—HUGH GARDEN

Above, right: The use of painted burlap above a wood wainscoting was often used at the turn of the century. Here, redwood is used for the wainscoting and the cutout pattern in a wall section at the Sun House in Ukiah, California. The pattern was designed and cut by the original owner of the house, Grace Hudson, a noted artist who painted Native Americans in the early part of the century.

Below: In a Berkeley, California, home, a painted frieze mural by San Francisco artist George Zaffle is set above stained douglas-fir wainscoting. Note how the sense of the space opening outwards is given by both the subject matter as well as by the transition from the lower darkness to upper lightness. It is almost as though one is looking out over a wall at the vista beyond.

Surface surrounds us. In the home, it is the part of the house that encompasses us, that defines the concepts of space talked about previously. Surface is what we look at, touch, sit upon, brush against, and walk on. And more than this, it is what we visually and tactilely depend upon to give cohesion and sense to the confines within which we live. In his 1911 book *Bungalows,* Henry Saylor began the chapter on "Interior Finish" by describing what he called "the simplest treatment of all, where the exterior is covered with rough boards," and the interior is the unadorned exposed studs and boards of the exterior. "Do not be content," he warned, "to have these appear just as the carpenter finds it convenient to place them; have them symmetrically spaced on either side of center openings, with the horizontal member forming the windowsills carried all the way around." If additional expense is allowed, he added, then the studs "…may be covered and the wall space can be painted or, better still, covered with a rough fabric in cool gray, apple green, or a pleasing shade of brown."

One finds here the key elements of surface in the Arts and Crafts interior: the emphasis upon the simple, the appreciation of nature by reference to color, the avoidance of sham, and, what is probably most important of all, the fact that each element of the interior, indeed of the entire home as described by Saylor, is achievable by the motivated amateur craftsman.

The desire for simplicity was in part a reaction to the clutter of the past decades. "We do not want fussy things to annoy us," Keith's magazine advised the housewife, "nor gaudy wall papers to shriek 'welcome' when we enter the room." But in another way, the quest for the simple was a larger backlash against the complexity of life at the turn of the century, against the new technologies and the new urbanized communities, against the new ways of making a living by factory work instead of by shop work. In 1830, more than nine Americans out of ten lived on

Louise Brigham wrote her book Box Furniture *in 1909 to provide an early example of recycling everyday materials in home-based craftwork and to illustrate allied interior-design ideals of the time. Her book provided how-to projects for everyday furniture pieces made from the wood boxes that were the equivalent of the brown-paper grocery bags of today.*

Above: Arts and Crafts wallpapers by Carol Mead, patterns adapted from period designs. Shown, from top to bottom, are oak leaves, daffodils, water weed, wild rose, irises, and lily pads.

Below, right: An exterior shingled wall of a Greene and Greene house in Pasadena, California.

new connections. The spread of the railroads, the web of the telegraph first and then the telephone, the growth of big business and mass marketing all tied the country together into a whirl and madness that left people with, as the cultural historian Jackson Lears has written, "...a feeling that life had become not only overcivilized but also curiously unreal."

Turning to nature and the outdoors, both for a renewed sense of healthfulness and for the motifs and colors in one's home, was an understandable response; it was both an inclusion of the outdoors in one's life and a return to a time when life was not so urbanized, when one lived in a more natural setting than the overpopulated cities of the turn of the century. One sought to place in one's life the muted sense of color that came from the outdoors, or as Stickley wrote, ". . . the varying tones of green, deep red, russet, and yellow of foliage, the soft wood browns with all their wide variations of modifying tones, the dim, rich colors found in rocks, and the gray-greens, yellow-greens, and deep blues of the ocean."

The call for honesty, for the avoidance of sham in both construction technique and material, was

the farm, made much of what they used, and worked according to the season; in 1930, nearly two-thirds of the population lived and worked in the industrialized city. Work became dictated by the time clock rather than by the season, and one bought what one needed rather than made it. People who had once lived in small, tightly knit farm communities, cut off from the world at large, made

Fireplace at Charles Fletcher Lummis's home, El Alisal, built between 1898 and 1910.

part of the reaction against the great amount of factory-made, machine-produced, ornamental scrollwork and molding that was used to decorate both the exterior and interior of Victorian homes. The poet and naturalist Charles Keeler, in his 1904 paean to simplicity, *The Simple Home,* wrote of the Victorian home as "quickly made and lightly abandoned." He described Victorian abodes as "petty makeshifts, to be sure, with imitation turrets, spires, porticoes, corbels, and elaborate bracket-work excrescences—palaces of crumbling plaster, with walls papered in gaudy patterns, and carpets of insolent device." The new kind of home he championed would be "simple and genuine." He would eliminate as much as possible "…all factory-made accessories in order that your dwelling may not be typical of American commercial supremacy, but rather of your fondness for things that

have been created as a response to your love of that which is good and simple and fit for daily companionship."

The creation of things by oneself was important. It brought meaning back into one's life, a meaning not met by the work of the factory or the work of the housewife. Handmade objects and hand-decorated surfaces could provide an expression of the self, even if the objects and surfaces themselves were handworked by others. As a result, hand-stitched curtains and bedspreads, stenciled walls, woven carpets, and woodcarved screens were advocated in such magazines as *House and Garden, The Ladies' Home Journal, House Beautiful,* and *The Craftsman.* These magazines brought a new concept of art into the home, an art of doing rather than an art of looking. Where once a family tried to raise its level of existence by hanging the colored lithographs of Nathaniel Currier and James

Variegated bricks were a popular material for fireplace construction around the turn of the century. This fireplace is in the 1911 Craftsman home number 104, constructed in New Jersey.

Charles A. Keeler (1871–1937), poet, naturalist, civic leader, and author of The Simple Home.

Merritt Ives on their walls, during this era the family members would sit in the evening appliquéing a linen table cover or hammering sheet brass into a candle shade. It was seen by many as a return to the home and hearthside, as a reinstatement of the home into one's life, and as part of the clarion call for the restoration of the family in a society gone astray.

EXTERIOR SURFACE

As the interior was meant to be expressive of the exterior, the exterior was intended to fit into and grow out of its setting. As Frank Lloyd Wright said in a 1902 speech to the Chicago Women's Club, "Make the walls of brick that the fire touched to tawny gold or ruddy tan, the choicest of all earth's hues. They will not rise rudely above the sod as through shot from beneath by a catapult, but recognize the surface of the ground on which they stand, gently spreading there to a substantial base that makes the building seem to stand more firmly in its socket in the earth and carry with a profile of grace the protection of its sheltering eaves." One sees this principle embodied in his early midwestern work that set the standards for what came to be called the Prairie School of architecture.

In the West, the brothers Charles and Henry Greene built homes that also embodied this principle, their work seeming to grow out of the earth—stones emerging from the greenery, graduating into the rough, distorted faces of the clinker bricks, and finally metamorphosing into the soft, human-scaled elegance and sophistication of their wooden Japanese-influenced structures.

In the East, exteriors were often in the shingle style, the rough wood stained to colors of the weathered grays of the Cape Cod beaches, or built, in appropriate landscapes, out of the materials of the earth: bricks, cement, and stucco. As Gustav Stickley wrote in *The Craftsman*, "A house that is built of stone where stones are in the fields, of concrete where the soil is sandy, of brick where brick can be had reasonably, or of wood if the house is in a mountainous wooded region, will from the beginning belong to the landscape. And the result is not only harmony but economy."

One of the original homes designed by Will Price in the Pennsylvania Rose Valley Community displays a handcrafted Mercer tile made at the Moravian Tile and Pottery Works in nearby Doylestown.

Both photos: At the Carmel, California, D. L. James house, designed by Charles Greene in 1918, the landscape and the building blend together into one unified whole. Formed from locally quarried rock, the house appears to grow naturally out of the cliff, emerging from the cliff with a transition so subtle that in places it is impossible to tell where the bedrock ends and the house begins.

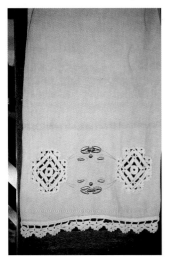

In this Berkeley, California, home, note how the textiles, carpets, and floral arrangement soften both the darkness of the room and hardness of the woodwork.

Textile piece from photo above.

INTERIOR WALLS

With interior walls, one finds again the emphasis on honesty, simplicity, nature, and craft. More often than not, walls were left with an image of plainness and simplicity. It was common to use such natural materials as untreated wood, bare or painted stucco, or burlap and canvas cloth stretched across wall panels. Often in the rooms in the front of the house—the den or library and the living room—woven wall coverings were used, or burlaps, Japanese grass cloth, and canvas. When painted with "subtle" colors, the surfaces seemed to give the wall a "…great depth and richness of color, as well as beauty of surface." They would give a feeling of repose to the room, a sense of quietude and peace.

In a 1908 *House Beautiful* article, one writer wrote of an interior that corresponded to "…the surroundings as perfectly as though the turf, the water of the lake, the leaves and bark of the trees, the mold of the wagon-road, had been carried to New York and matched in shops." It

A Sierra Madre, California, home displays various heights of wainscoting in the entry, living room, and dining room.

was important to bring nature into the home—both by motif and material—but only the genuine item. Artifice and imitation were scorned. Wallpapers that imitated wood were called by one writer "quite as vicious as imitation jewels." The popular practices in the past of wood graining and marbleizing, trompe l'oeil techniques of simulating wood or stone with paint, had no place in the Arts and Crafts home.

Stencils on the wall not only blend with artwork but can serve as a frame. Stencil by Helen Foster.

The "Pendant Frieze" stencil by Helen Foster.

Helen Foster's "Rose Trio" stencil pattern forms a frieze around this room.

STENCILS

In a sense, it would not be a far reach to see stenciling as the craftsman's wallpaper. Indeed, in some ways, both wallpaper and stencils had the same origins in the age-old drive to decorate one's wall surface with image and pattern. However, wallpaper evolved to high decor, while stencils verged on the common. Their divergence can almost be seen in the same spirit that we see the separation that occurred between the fine arts and the applied arts—the separation that formed the eventual impetus for the Arts and Crafts movement.

Stencils were often sold by mail order through advertisements in the popular home magazines, ready-cut patterns supplied with instructions and paints in approved colors. Sherwin-Williams, in their book on stencils, stated three principles to wall stenciling. First, the stencil must conform to the general scheme of the room design and color; second, it must look restful to the eyes; and third, the stencil pattern must form a "perfect background" for pictures to be hung. Usually on stucco walls, or burlaps, the home craftsman was told to repeat the lightly colored silhouette of a motif like a frieze along the

An example of conventionalized moths in the "Luna Frieze" stencil by Helen Foster.

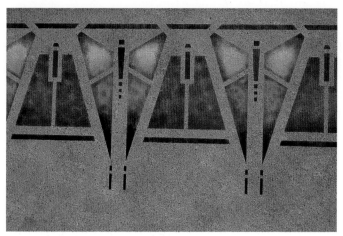

picture rail or under the wainscoting line instead of wood. "Whatever you do," advised one manual, "avoid overdoing, remember that the point is to get away and stay away from over-decoration."

Stencils can be applied directly onto a stucco or cloth wall, or to cotton, linen, burlap, or grass cloth, and then tacked on or taken off the wall according to the season. In any case, oil-based paint should be used, thinned with turpentine so that the colors don't shout at the inhabitants. A little bit of shading inside the same color, although difficult to execute, helps the patterns look more grounded to the wall surface rather than looking as though they were pasted on like stickers.

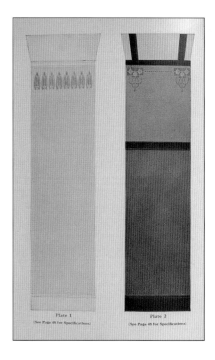

A 1915 example of a Sherwin Williams color modulation chart from The ABC of Home Painting.

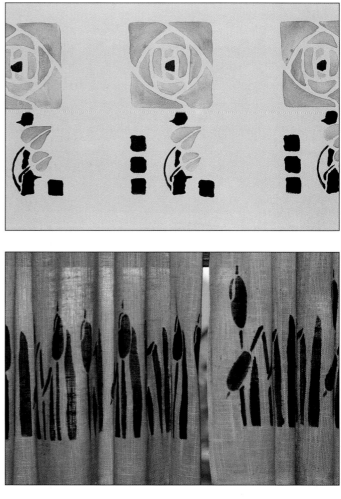

Showing application of a two-color stencil to a wall, Helen Foster recommends that "soft coloring is more appropriate to the period."

Top: The "Rose" stencil pattern by Charles Rennie Mackintosh.

Bottom: These linen curtains with a cattail motif display another application for stencils.

Attractive built-in cupboards from Craftsman home number 85 demonstrate Craftsman woodworking at its finest.

WOOD

Wood was without question the quintessential material of the Arts and Crafts interior. It was natural with rare exception, abundant, and, compared to wallpaper, was believed to be more sanitary. Charles Keeler wrote bluntly that "my own preference for the interior walls of a wooden house is wood," and specifically, as he explained, "…the natural California redwood…rubbed with a wax

dressing to preserve the natural color, or left to darken without any preservative." When not left in their natural state, as Keeler would prefer, hardwoods such as oak and chestnut were often stained or fumed with ammonia. Since oak and chestnut contained tannic acid, when exposed to ammonia, they reached a "mellow darkness of hue that formerly was supposed to come from age alone," as Gustav Stickley wrote. The process of fuming was discovered, according to Stickley, when "some oak boards stored in a stable in England were found after a time to have taken on a beautiful mellow brown tone," as a result of the ammonia fumes from the urine naturally found in stables. Fuming interior woodwork was difficult though, and not advised, both because of the danger of the process

The woodwork on the walls and ceiling of this bungalow is stained a greenish gray, contrasting with the brown stain of the floor. Note how the furniture, by its wood construction and stain, becomes part of the room's design rather than isolated elements. Ornament is spare in this room—one vase of flowers, several Navajo rugs—as though a testament to the benefits of the simple life.

and because of the lack of predictability of the results. Stickley wrote in *The Craftsman* how interior woodwork could be fumed by shutting up the room to be done, "…stuffing up all the crevices as if for fumigating with sulphur, and then setting around on the floor a liberal number of dishes into which the ammonia is poured last of all." He adds the warning onto this that "the person pouring the ammonia should get out of the room as quickly as possible after the fumes are released."

An idealized illustration of a child's room of the period using fairy tales as a theme. The example shows how the walls can be divided into panels, in this case by woodwork stained in light green. The lower panels provide scenes that give a sense of opening the room outwards into a playful, naturalistic world; whereas, the middle panels provide almost a friezelike effect on the wall.

Because of the lack of tannin, woods other than chestnut and oak did not take to fuming. Stickley recommended that woods such as rock elm or brown ash be treated to a very light stain of either brown, gray, or green. With cypress, he suggested treatment with sulfuric acid to achieve an effect similar to the Japanese practice of burying the wood, which brought the wood to the desired color, "…a soft gray-brown against which the markings stand out strongly." The treatment was an application of diluted sulfuric acid (one-to-five ratio with water) directly to the surface of the wood, which was then allowed to dry thoroughly before a final finish was added. The sulfuric acid method, in a stronger (one-to-three) solution, also worked on red birch, which would fade in color if left untreated. Stickley recommended maple or beech be finished in a gray tone, "…as this harmonizes admirable with the colors most often used in a daintily furnished room,—such as dull blue, old rose, pale straw color, reseda green and old ivory." The gray finish was achieved by brushing a weak solution of iron rust on the wood, a solution made by "throwing iron filings, rusty

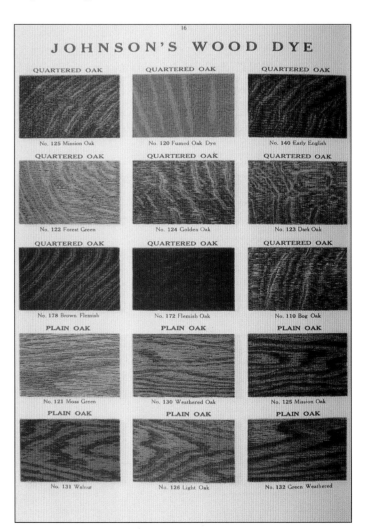

A chart of wood dyes for use in the home and how-to advice from the Arts and Crafts period.

In the 1902 Berkeley house designed by Bernard Maybeck for George Boke, the interior is entirely made of unpainted redwood.

nails, or any small pieces of iron into acid vinegar or a weak solution of acetic acid. After a couple of days, the solution should be strained off and diluted with water until it is of the strength needed to get the desired color upon the wood." The color achieved is not seen until the wood is thoroughly dry, at which point it should be sandpapered and given a coat of thin, slightly darkened shellac and then rubbed with wax.

Wood provided more than texture for the wall surface; it often provided the means of creating rhythm in the interior space. When used as panels for wainscoting or in strips to break either the dado or the entire wall into panels, like stencils, it created repetitious patterns in the room that gave a rhythmical accent to the room. Between rooms, especially rooms that opened one onto another, the rhythmic pattern created could tie the separate spaces into a unified whole. This idea of wainscoting was a distinct move away from the heavy panels of carved wood popular with earlier stylists. It could, and often was, as simple as "…wood strips over a textile wall covering."

• *1. Some variations in conventionalization that are based on the nasturtium.* • *2-3. Examples of variations upon conventionalized patterns based upon plant forms are from* The Use of the Plant in Decorative Design for High Schools, *1912.* • *4. Highly conventionalized flower and dragonfly motifs are repeated in slight variations to create a pleasing wallpaper pattern. Arts and Crafts design expert Tim Hansen explains that the use of a pattern as a repeat panel in a frieze border around a room can create a rhythm and flow, treating space as something alive and encouraging the viewer's eyes to move around the room.* • *5. This detail of a fireplace is from Greene and Greene's 1909 Blacker House.*

MOTIFS

Inspiration for Arts and Crafts stencils, wallpaper, and furniture-cutout patterns came mostly from nature—plants, animals, insects, and landscapes. Rather than copying these forms directly, craftspeople and designers of the period took the images of nature, and in the terminology of the day, "conventionalized" them. Conventionalization was a design technique widely taught at schools and used not only for home decoration but for book design, magazine advertising, and general graphic motifs. It was a technique used to express natural forms in decorative terms by the "perfecting of the shape, the grasping of essential elements, the omission of uninteresting or unimportant detail," as Maude Lawrence wrote in *The Use of the Plant in Decorative Design for High Schools,* 1912. As the influential teacher, designer, and tilemaker Ernest Batchelder wrote in his key work, *Design in Theory and Practice,* "The closer nature is brought to the abstract, the less essential it is to keep to any particular, recognized form." He was quick to add, though, that "nothing could

be more stupid than the mere repetition at regular intervals of a naturalistic insect."

When such a conventionalized motif is designed, the goal is to achieve a harmony within a room or the house by repeating the motif—using it as a pattern for a frieze along a wall, as embroidery for a pillow, a pattern in the carpet, or a stencil on a table runner, giving the Arts and Crafts house a rhythmic unity. Frank Lloyd Wright, for example, repeated the hollyhock design in his famed Hollyhock House in Los Angeles. Wright designed not only concrete columns and walls with the pattern, but also used the conventionalized geometric hollyhock shape in the stained glass, the mantelpiece, and for the furniture he designed for the house. When well planned, a repeated use of a motif can achieve a sense of movement within a room and between rooms. In the words of Tim Hansen, a Craftsman carpenter and an expert in Arts and Crafts design in Berkeley, California, "It must have a sense of rhythm, and it must have the movement, to carry the eye from one unit to the next."

COLOR

The Arts and Crafts movement fostered a new sensitivity towards colors, a turn towards subtle colors that some identified with the delicate hues of Japanese wood-block prints. Harvey Ellis, one of the most brilliant artist-designers of the movement, wrote in *The Craftsman,* "We shall find aid in our problem in the simple, restrained color schemes found in the better Japanese color prints. Here we have colors of the utmost subtlety combined frankly with that delicate appreciation of the intimate relations of tones."

This quest for new color came about partially as a result of the change in the technology of paint and dye making during the late nineteenth century, a change which made ready-mix paints available

Japanese wood-block prints such as this one by Hiroshige were available in America before the turn of the century and served as inspiration to many designers of the Arts and Crafts movement. Some praised the simplicity of form; others valued the combination of subtle colors.

The entrance to the Warren Hile bungalow in Sierra Madre, California, painted a "Spanish moss" green, is balanced by naturally stained wood on the door and sidelights. The Greene and Greene-style lighting is by Arroyo Craftsman.

The great art teacher and wood-block artist Arthur Wesley Dow was introduced to Japanese art through a book containing examples of Hokusai's work. Inspired by the subtle colorations and asymmetrical design, he and another important oriental-art critic in Boston, Ernest Fenollosa, developed a system of art education that strongly influenced design concepts across the country at the turn of the century. This picture from his often-reprinted book, Composition, *shows examples of how the synthesis of line, color, and the Japanese concept of notan, balancing of light and darkness, are necessary in composing good design.*

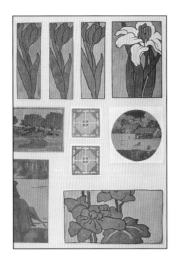

from the 1880s. Having easy access not only to these colors, but to their different intensities and shades enabled homeowners of the period to indulge their fancies with combinations of color and gradations that had been previously reserved only for experts. Sample cards, not unlike the color test strips available from paint stores today, also became available, offering a better chance to preview colors and tones before applying the paintbrush to the wall.

During this period, there was much systematic study of color by experts, especially as to its effect upon the home and the occupants within. Many household advisors turned to the work of Michel Eugene Chevreul (1786–1889), the Director of Dyes for the Gobelins tapestry works in France, who, for the first time, systematically recorded a system of "laws of colors" in his seminal work, *The Principles of Harmony and Contrast of Colors,* published in 1839. Not only did he put into writing the fact that complementary colors placed side by side in a pattern appear more intense, but he also pointed out that two colors adjacent to one another, but not complements, will appear to be altered in hue. For example, when red is placed next to orange, it appears as purplish red next to yellowish orange.

Candace Wheeler, the textile artist, likened color to sound. Since strict rules apply to constructing music with major and minor scales, she argued, similar rules should apply to color. "The musician, " she wrote, "has gathered

Using colors found in nature, here drawn from the colors of the butterfly, color combinations can be made that are not only pleasing and harmonious but that also relate to the natural world outside.

his tones from every audible thing in nature—and fitted and assorted and built them into a science; and why should not some painter who is also a scientist take the many variations of colour which lie open to his sight, and range and fit, and combine, and write the formula?"

In practical application, like skirt lengths for women, popular color combinations changed decade by decade. While tertiary color combinations were dominate in the 1880s, the tendency in later decades was to move toward more secondary and primary color combinations. Looking at the period literature, we can find two main types of color combinations: complementary and monochromatic. A typical complementary combination would be an olive green paired with the color of redwoods or a deep grayish blue with a sandy yellow. In a monochromatic scheme, all the colors in a room would be a variation upon one dominant color, differing by gradation and intensity.

The living room and the den generally took a heavier color than the rest of the house, an attitude of quiet and comfortable repose being sought after. In the bedroom, kitchen, breakfast nook, and bathroom, it was believed that lighter, if not pastel colors, were appropriate. This had to do with the belief among advocates of the new style of housing that white was the color of sanitation, that it must have a good effect upon one's health and mental well-being and, would therefore be appropriate for those areas of the home where the woman of the house performed her work.

A color harmony circle shows how secondary, tertiary, and quaternary colors are created from the primary colors. Notice how the complementary colors are incorporated into the floral patterns.

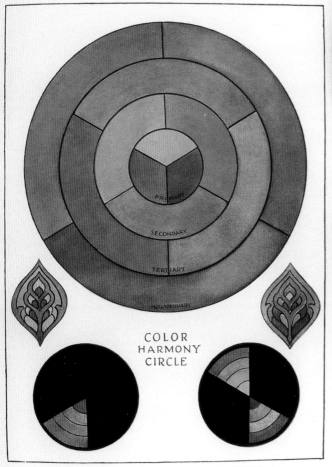

COMPLEMENTARY COLOR WHEEL — COLOR CHART NO. 1

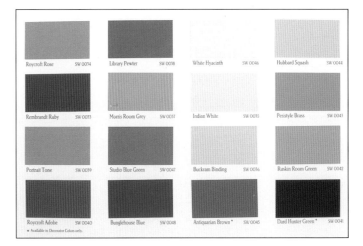

In 1991, Roycroft Associates teamed up with the Sherwin-Williams Company to develop a color palette called Roycroft Arts and Crafts Colors. The colors were based upon research done in both the Sherwin-Williams archives and at the Roycroft campus in East Aurora, New York.

ON THE FLOOR

In homes associated with the Arts and Crafts movement, it mattered less what the floors were made of and more what was put on them. Floors of hardwood, tile, and in some cases concrete, were almost always partially covered with carpets, mats, and rugs. With the opening up of the interior, these floor coverings could be used to further define the spaces—a small oriental carpet in an inglenook, a handwoven rug in front of a settle. Further, the hues of color or the patterns used in stencils or curtains could be repeated in the carpet or rug to create a stronger harmony within the room and further delineate the space.

Floor coverings ranged from the oriental carpet, which had been popular since the nineteenth century, to both machine-made and handmade rugs. In general, the majority of rugs at this time were woven on power looms by American manufacturers. The common types were Ingrain, Brussels, Wilton, Velvet, and Axminster; made from wool, linen, cotton, hemp, or jute. Also popular were the Japanese or Chinese grass mats made from native grasses. The more well-to-do, however, could always commission a carpet design from Morris and Company.

It was during the Arts and Crafts movement that the hand-woven rug saw a remarkable resurgence. Candace Wheeler recorded the growing interest and popularity of these rugs and the associated newly budding home industries. She advocated village women take up the task of hand-making rugs as a way of running a profitable home business.

On the other hand, weaving rugs as a hobby was extremely popular. As Mabel Tuke Priestman noted in 1910, "It is now a number of years since the revival of hand-weaving in America," and Henrietta Keith took note of a California woman who made a "wonderfully handsome rug" with long brown hair taken from her horse. These handmade rugs varied from a simple crochet to fancy hand-loomed works, and made use of materials from a rustic hemp to cut-up rags. For color, Priestman advocated the use of natural dyes made from numerous roots, barks, and bog plants as an alternative to the artificial color of the aniline dyes. Such colors, she noted, would harmonize with the natural tones of the interior.

Above: A 1912 sampler of rugs considered appropriate for homes of the period.

The "Magnolia" pattern carpet, handcrafted by Nancy Thomas at the Blue Hills Studio.

Carpet designed and produced by JAX rugs.

Lit by shower lights, the dining room in this Berkeley, California, home uses a combination of "Avalon" pattern wallpaper for the field, the "Apple Tree" frieze above, and a ceiling trim of the "Apple Tree" border above the wood wainscotting. All wallpapers are by Bradbury and Bradbury Art Wallpapers.

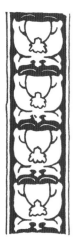

WALLPAPER

Some wallpapers with the correct sense of color and motif were adopted by the Arts and Crafts movement, especially in its earlier incarnations of the movement and generally more on the Eastern Seaboard, where the influence of the more decorative English Arts and Crafts movement was felt. But they did not take over the room as in earlier times; rather, they were used as a fill between the dado and the frieze or for the frieze above a plain papered or clothed fill. The patterns also altered with the times. No more were classical renderings used, columns and flutings, nor was there a realistic trompe l'oeil imitation of nature, of the lushness of foliage and flower; patterns became more stylized and geometric, the shapes of nature were abstracted, conventionalized.

But it was difficult to reconcile wallpaper with the movement. It was only after wallpaper stopped being handmade and was mass manufactured earlier in the nineteenth century that it became affordable for any but the extreme upper class. Wallpaper, unlike most other elements of the Arts and Crafts home, was not an item that could be produced at home if needed, and therefore could not convey any element of the owner in the house, any element of the drive to do-it-yourself, to put oneself into the home.

The "Thistle" wallpaper pattern as produced by Bradbury and Bradbury.

A frieze area that has been panelized, the width between the panels determined by the box beams above. The field area below the picture rail is the "Apple Tree" frieze, decoupaged over "Glenwood" wallpaper with a companion border above the wainscot. Wallpapers by Bradbury and Bradbury Art Wallpapers.

LIGHT

The dining room in Frank Lloyd Wright's Oak Park home was added in 1895. Wright's arrangement of the ceiling and bay windows was ingenious for a time when candles and oil lamps were the standard and electric lights still a novelty. A writer in an 1897 House Beautiful *article described the room, declaring that "there is not a bulb in sight, but set into a ceiling and actually part of it is a screen of intricate pattern, covered with a thin paper. The light is turned on above and filters through much subdued."*

LIGHT, LIKE LIFE, IS AS WE MAKE IT. It may be a thing of parts, a source of comfort, an inspiring influence, an element of the beautiful, or it may be as it is today just a part of things—in the utilitarian sense a 'servant in the house' —nothing more. —F. LAURENT GODINEG, *THE LIGHTING BOOK,* 1913

It is light that gives depth to our union of space and surface, that allows us to discover the home we live in. By controlling it, we can restrain the intrusion of the daytime; by using it, we can overcome the night. A soft sunshine filtered through curtains will give to a window seat a feeling of peaceful rest. A candle

Candleholders and a vase were made by Van Briggle Pottery between 1910 and 1915. Artus van Briggle, the founder of the pottery, had been a decorator for the Rookwood Pottery before beginning his own pottery in 1901. The Art Nouveau influence on his work came from the three years he spent in Paris studying under a scholarship from Rookwood.

flickering, the light of a kerosene lamp, the glow of a gas lamp, the aura cast by firelight, all will bring us reminders of the warmth of gathered family and friends.

Lighting in Arts and Crafts homes was subdued and restful. Compared to Victorian homes, where strong gas light and the new incandescent light bulbs shone their harsh light upon the brilliantly colored walls, Arts and Crafts homes shied away from direct lights, seeking instead to create many layers of light using a number of different methods. For shades, they used materials such as mica, iridescent glass, cloth, and woven baskets, all of which not only dampened the harshness of the bare bulbs but gave the warm glow to the room so desired. Also, as the outdoors were encouraged to be part of the house, natural light was sought as a source of illumination where possible. Instead of the heavy draperies of the Victorian days, thin canvas, cotton, or linen curtains were hung across the windows, allowing abundant sunlight to come through.

A TIME OF CHANGE: THE TECHNOLOGY OF LIGHTING

The Arts and Crafts movement converged with the turn of the century, a time of vast technological changes.

In October of 1879, Thomas Edison discovered the secret of achieving a sustained period of incandescent lighting, and not only did the method of lighting the home begin to change, but the whole sense of light in the home underwent a transformation. This new way of lighting started first in the public buildings, spreading next to the homes of the wealthy, and only then finally reaching the homes of the millions. The old methods of achieving light, kerosene and gas, declined after Edison's invention, but even in 1899, still 75 percent of homes were using gas for illumination. Even by 1919, gas was still being used by 21 percent. Because of this, period fixtures that were made for both gas and electricity were called "gasolier-electroliers."

These changes in the technology of lighting were translated into other constructions of lighting devices with different demands. While kerosene lamps and candles

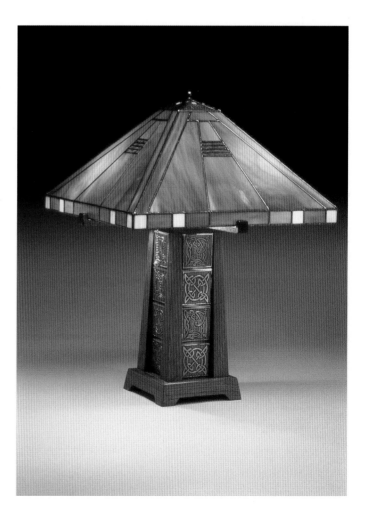

This Foursquare lamp was made by Raymond Tillman, a contemporary craftsman.

"Beauty is never secured when one looks directly at the electric light. The lamps should be so turned that their direct rays strike the ceiling only. Then the softened, reflected light reveals and creates beauty everywhere."

—CHARLES F. EATON

were movable, gas and electric lighting needed stationary points since their source of energy, or light, came through a tube or wires in the wall. The idea of lighting, therefore, changed from something one could carry throughout the house, from room to room as needed, to something well planned out and set permanently in place.

In these new lighting devices, the very characteristics of the fuel determined the aesthetic design possibilities. For example, the shape of the kerosene lamp was largely determined by its basin, having as it did the necessity of holding sufficient kerosene oil to burn. Gas fixtures, on the other hand, needed to be connected to the walls by pipes that restricted movement and needed to be taken into design consideration. Electric lamps were, compared to the first two, less restricted since their wires were loose and could even be hidden at times. No longer restricted by the gas-pipe pendants, one of the new popular designs were chain-suspended electric bulbs called "showers."

Part of the slowness in the transformation to electricity was a resistance to it by the general populace. Outlandish myths persisted, such as the one that electric light would cause freckles. Fires, explosions, and electrocution caused by the new form of lighting were widely talked and written about. Especially disliked was the harsh illumination of incandescent light at the turn of the century. One author alarmed, "Whether in the home, the office or the factory, the pernicious, devastating effect of these over-brilliant, unmodified light sources is the

In this Pasadena home designed by the architects Greene and Greene, the shower light was designed and constructed by James Ipekjian of the James Randell Company.

Lit by both candlelight and by the natural pouring in of light through the windows, there is a sense of calm and repose in the sanctuary of the San Francisco Swedenborgian Church. Built in 1894, this simple church was designed in a collaboration between Pastor Joseph Worcester and the architectural office of A. Page Brown.

growing cause of much untold misery and suffering, generally attributed to other innocent causes." This writer advocated lighting fixtures that would soften the effect of this new, harsh lighting—fixtures that would keep the feeling of a softer light of times gone by. One technique undertaken to overcome the problem of harsh light was the use of stained glass. Fulper Pottery, for example, produced mushroom lamps from 1910, using shades made of molded clay and glaze with stained glass inset in irregular forms. Another decorative technique was glass shades with frosted surfaces that were hand painted. Occasionally, even indirect illumination was attempted to soften this new severe form of lighting.

A kiosk table lamp reminiscent of gas lanterns of old, handcrafted by the current-day craftsperson Raymond Tillman.

MATERIALS FOR LIGHTING

MICA

Mica is an orange, half-transparent, thin mineral silicate that is found naturally and peels easily into thin sheets. Used extensively by Dirk van Erp for his copper lamp shades after 1910 and by the Roycrofters for their lighting, it gives a warm glow that is reminiscent of candlelight. Since it is nonflammable, it is appropriate material for lamp shades. Sometimes, mica used during the Arts and Crafts period was also called "isinglass."

GLASS

Versatile and adaptable, this form of melted sand comes transmuted in a number of forms: mold-blown glass is made by blowing glass into a two-part mold; mouth-blown glass is made without a mold and thereby can retain the appeal of imperfections of bubbles and waves. Pressed glass, made by squeezing glass between two steel molds, is very costly. Sheet glass comes in a diversity of colors and is most often used for stained-glass production. Bent glass is made by heating glass and then molding it over a form. Once glass is formed, further applications such as frosting, etching, and stenciling can adapt its appearance to give the desired quality of light to the user.

SHELLS

Because of the translucent quality of shells, a number of Arts and Crafts craftspeople used them for lamp shades. Charles Frederick Burton and his daughter Elizabeth Burton in California were famed for their use of "abalone, melon, and Philippine shells, to produce lamps and sconces in floral forms." Shells were used in their wholeness or carefully peeled into layers to form sheets that almost gave the impression of sheet glass.

• *1. A wicker and cloth lamp shade tops the copper base of this lamp found in the log house at Craftsman Farm.* • *2. This copper lamp with mica shade casts a warm light that enhances the dark Burma teakwood of the Gamble House entry hall.* • *3. A paper and wood lampshade provides a soft glow on the van Briggle vase.* • *4. The soft green of the Tiffany lamp shade and the matte green finish of the Grueby vase bring a cool naturalness to the warmth of the wood, metal, and tile of Greene and Greene's Duncan Irwin House in Pasadena.* • *5. A Fulper buttressed vase was used in the construction of this attractive lamp.* • *6. The light coming through this Tiffany lamp shade made of shell adds a warm glow to the tabletop. The vase is by the Rookwood Pottery.* • *7. A Tiffany lamp.*

Lit by windows in the stairwell, one walks upwards in light to the grand living room on the second floor of the Weeks Lodge in Lancaster, New Hampshire.

CLOTH

Often used in solid colors, cloth was used to eliminate the unwanted glare of electric lights. The materials used varied widely, especially when made by the average home seamstress. The materials included grass cloth, cretonne, cotton, silk, brocade, taffeta, and satin. With his wicker lamp shades, Gustav Stickley went so far as to use the exotic solid habutae silk cloth from Japan.

FILTERED LIGHT

There are infinite possibilities to the householder who has what is called the artistic instinct and the leisure and willingness to experiment, and experiments need not be limited to prints or to cottons, for wonderful combinations of colour are possible in silks where light is called in as an influence in the composition.

In my own country-house, I have used the two strongest colours—red and blue—in this doubled way, with delightful effect. The blue, which is the face colour, presenting long, pure folds of blue, with warmed reddish shadows between, while at sunset, when the rays of light are level, the variations are like a sunset sky.
—PRINCIPLES OF HOME DECORATION,
CANDACE WHEELER

Chinese and Japanese imported pottery was extremely popular during this period and as much as 75 percent of the imports were used to make the popular lamps.

WOVEN MATERIALS

Wicker, bamboo, and other woven materials, including grasses, were often used in lamp shades made during the Arts and Crafts period. With some of the styles, a distinct reference was made to the handicrafts of the Native Americans. With others, the feeling was given of the outdoor life, especially when used with wicker furniture on a front porch or sleeping porch.

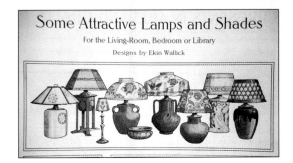

Rather than the looped and festooned curtains of the Victorian period, the "long folds of the straight hanging curtain," as Candace Wheeler described them, became favored from the turn of the century onward. The effect was to give the windows, and thereby the outdoors, more prominence while decreasing the import of the curtains. Curtains became valued not for their effect as tapestries, but for their ability to filter light, for their ability to increase a sense of openness and a commune with nature. Windows were there to let in an abundance of light and fresh air—and curtains, as contrasted with the layers of rich, heavy draperies of the Victorian interiors, were there to enhance the view, not to block it. As Wheeler wrote, "The simpler the treatment, the better the effect."

The materials chosen for these curtains tended to be the lighter, more simple and inexpensive fabrics—fabrics such as "printed cotton, English Chintz, taffeta or dimity,

An abundance of sunlight, softened and diffused by a thin curtain, gives a room a sense of restfulness and comfort. The curtain and pillow in the photograph above are by Arts and Crafts Period Textiles.

domestic or French cretonne, East India cotton, and Chinese or Japanese cottons and crepes" could be used. Candace Wheeler, in her *Principles of Home Decoration*, praised the graceful quality of silk, for its "tenacity of tint and flexibility of substance," despite its cost. Cottons and linens could make inexpensive hangings, except they were inhospitable to dyes. Today textile artists, such as Dianne Ayres and Ann Wallace, offer curtains and curtain fabrics that emphasize these qualities referring to this past era, using materials that are simply woven, durable, and sometimes even rough in feel.

In choosing to decorate with curtains, color is an important consideration. Not only does color in curtain fabric unite and enhance the harmony of the room, it alters the look of the room when the light is filtered through it. As Wheeler explains, "If the room is dark or cold in its exposure, to hang the windows with sun-colored silk or muslin will cheat the eye and imagination into the idea that it is a sunny room." Materials as lightweight as transparent silk or colored scrim can be used in this way to color the light that enters through the window. As written in a *Craftsman* article about Stickley and his Craftsman Farm's Log House: "The light is softened to a mellow glow by the casement curtains of burnt orange with a border worked in appliqué linen."

The last considerations, but not the least, are the

In this living-room shot from The Craftsman, *the mustard-yellow curtain not only gives a warmth to the light that comes through the windows, but also adds a vivid color accent to the room.*

In the 1904 San Diego Marston House by Irving Gill, light shining onto the daybed is filtered by the first set of curtains or more completely blocked when the second set are closed. The embroidered pillow is by Dianne Ayres of Arts and Crafts Period Textiles.

patterns on curtains. Should they be plain or patterned? In simple bungalow interiors associated with *The Craftsman* where walls and woodwork are plain, stencil-patterned curtains or printed cottons can add a positive decorative element. Though, when the walls are papered, plain material is preferable. Motifs on the walls, however, can complement when repeated on a curtain fabric as in the example presented from the 1910 Sherwin-Williams Company book *Your Home and Its Decoration*.

What's most important is to reach a balance between light and shading. Light should be plenty, one writer wrote for *House Beautiful* in 1898, and "…is wanted in a house, but it should be softened and diffused." It needs to be filtered. We, living now at the end of the twentieth

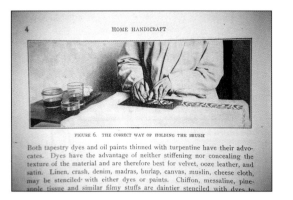

HOME HANDICRAFT

FIGURE 6.   THE CORRECT WAY OF HOLDING THE BRUSH

Both tapestry dyes and oil paints thinned with turpentine have their advocates. Dyes have the advantage of neither stiffening nor concealing the texture of the material and are therefore best for velvet, ooze leather, and satin. Linen, crash, denim, madras, burlap, canvas, muslin, cheese cloth, may be stenciled with either dyes or paints. Chiffon, messaline, pineapple tissue and similar filmy stuffs are daintier stenciled with dyes to

Curtains, pillows, and table runners can be stenciled just as easily as walls. This 1908 picture from The Good Housekeeping Manual of Home Handicrafts *is a demonstration of the use of short, round brushes best suited for this work.*

century, are more accustomed to the attitude that the bigger the windows, the brighter and better they are. But there is much to be said for this hundred-year-old attitude of appreciation of the subtle illumination that could be afforded by the filtering of light.

The curtains in this mock-up design will be appliquéd and embroidered when finished. This exclusive design was adapted by Dianne Ayres of Arts and Crafts Period Textiles from a stained-glass panel found in a northern California home.

COLORED LIGHT

Like curtains, stained glass also functioned as a diffuser of natural light. It was, in a sense, a curtain of glass that allowed the light through. It functioned also as a barricade to unsightly scenes outside. From the 1876 domestic collaboration of H. H. Richardson and John La Farge on the William Watts Sherman house of Newport, Rhode Island, to numerous small bungalows built after the turn of the century, stained glass was chosen as a way to improve the aesthetic appeal of a window.

Various American artisans and architects took advantage of the

technological advances being made in this medium. Frank Lloyd Wright developed his geometric designs from approximately 1902 that, philosophically suited as they were to his approach to architecture, were especially suited for machine production. Steam-powered rolling machinery now permitted a more efficient manufacture of larger panes of glass and of opalescent glass, a machine-rolled milky kind introduced in the 1870s. It could now be set within stiff zinc cames—a method that reduced the danger of buckling. All of this eliminated the need for the great amounts of bracing that was traditional and allowed for thinner windows. These new methods also reduced the costs of the conventional methods by about half, allowing the spread of "Wright-inspired" stained glass throughout the Midwest, for example.

The traditional method of the stained-glass art as practiced by Morris and Company is a complex craft. A watercolor sketch, called

A stained-glass window designed by Greene and Greene for one of their masterful Pasadena homes. The glasswork of the Greenes is famous for the expressive, almost sculptural black outlines that were achieved by mounting up and chiseling away the lead.

the "cartoon," is first prepared for the window. Then various sheets of glass in "manifold colors—greens, blues, reds—one shade flowing into another, one color veining another like marble, one hue changing to many variegated hues" are cut along the black outline of the watercolor figure to form the small pieces of the glass puzzle. After all the pieces are cut, glazier is wrapped around each piece. Then, to secure the joints, lead cames varying from one-sixteenth inch to one-half inch are put on adjacent glass pieces, which only then are soldered with a tin and lead mix.

The difficulty in this craft is that glass changes character dramatically as the light shines through it, changing not only by the time of day but by the very position of the viewer. Each sheet of glass has its

Natural light filters delicately through the work of contemporary stained-glass artist Randell Wright of Wright Design.

The entrance hall at the Pasadena Gamble House is a masterpiece of Japonisme romanticism blended into the turn-of-the-century aesthetic of Craftsman simplicity. The finger joints at the foot of the staircase are so exaggerated that, though in principle an oriental technique, in practice it becomes a style unique to architect brothers Greene and Greene. The Greene brothers dreamed of visiting Japan or China, but they never did.

Right: The century-old Judson Stained Glass Studio was involved from the beginning with the southern California Arts and Crafts movement. Not only was William Lee Judson the founder of the studio and an organizing member of the Guild of Arroyo Craftsmen, but his studio was the location for the guild. Still in existence today, it is being run by fourth-and-fifth generation members of the Judson family.

Far Right: Some sorted stained-glass pieces ready for use at the Judson Stained Glass Studio.

Below: In the San Francisco Swedenborgian Church, the stained glass, by Bruce Porter, refers back to the garden outside the church and to the world of nature rather than taking on an overtly religious theme.

own distinct character, from a smooth or wrinkled surface to a granulated or rippled one, not to mention all the intensities of colors. So, if allowances are not carefully made, a piece of thin glass may look like a hole while a dense-colored piece may appear to be a blot. One way to overcome this problem is by plating, which is literally to place one plate of glass over another until the desired intensity of color is achieved. The brother architects Greene and Greene used this plating method to its fullest, creating a new three-dimensional style of stained glass that they used in many of the high-art lighting fixtures.

THE CRAFT OF LIGHTING

The beauty of metal when used in lighting fixtures is in the warmth of the light reflected off the hammered surfaces. Two of the most favored materials in the Arts and Crafts lexicon—copper and brass—were used, because of their malleability, to make shades for lights. A number of methods were employed, such as hammering, making cutouts, soldering pieces together, or, especially with copper, etching a design or pattern. Although the art of Dirk van Erp's hand-hammering required a highly sophisticated level of skill and technique, many lamps made were easy enough for amateurs to copy at home. Gustav Stickley in *The Craftsman* wrote about his lamp designs that "each and every one could be made at home by any amateur who has gained some skill in

Exterior lighting, as designed by Greene and Greene for the Pasadena Duncan Irwin house, became part of the architecture of the building by its reference to Japanese lanterns, adding a distinctive oriental touch to the home.

Shower lights, with shades in a graceful floral form, provide a dispersed even light for those dining beneath. Here the lights are hung above the dining table in the Duncan Irwin house designed by Greene and Greene.

Hanging lanterns work in conjunction with table lights to create an even radiance of light in the Craftsman Farm log house.

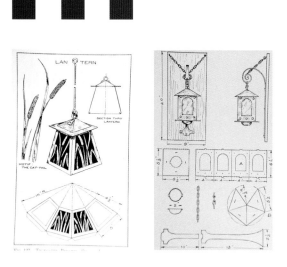

From the same book, illustrations for a hanging lamp with a cattail motif and a cylindrical hanging lamp with mica or art glass. These drawings were to provide models for home-handcrafters doing metalwork.

working with metals." With a beautifully aged patina and the mellow color gained by firing, it was the homeliness and the primitive quality of copper and brass that was best thought to fit well into the Arts and Crafts interior.

THE USE OF LIGHT

Light attracts people. Even in a comfortably lit room, people have the tendency to sit closest to the well-lit area and shy away from the shadowy corners. Brightness of light indicates activity; a more subdued level of lighting can lead one into a mood of contemplation.

There is a tendency to want to have one large lighting fixture when an even level of illumination throughout a room is desired; but the same effect, as was often illustrated in *The Craftsman*, can be achieved by placing small lighting fixtures in diverse locations throughout the room. This technique works well, especially in rooms with high ceilings.

One of the more difficult areas of the home to light is the dining room. When eating, we want attention directed to the food and the guests gathered for the meal. A light hung low over the dining table can focus the dining crowd upon the table and each other, but it must be carefully adjusted. As the diagram shows, a hanging fixture should not be so low as to prevent eye contact with other people around the table, yet it should be low enough so that the bare bulbs do not glare into the diners' eyes. When electricity was still new, one alarmed writer warned his readers that "many a case of indigestion has resulted from constant nightly exposure of overstrained eyes and nerves to the insidious glare of exposed lights above the dining table."

If the dome type of dining-room chandelier is too heavy in appearance, a more playful approach may be taken with a "shower" light. This style of lighting was,

This example of shower lights above a dining-room table was published in the 1912 Book of Home Building and Decoration.

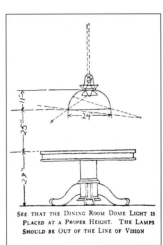

As illustrated in this 1913 guide to the new innovation of electrical lighting, the harshness of bare bulbs should not shine into people's eyes but rather should be redirected to cast a pool of light onto a surface where focused attention is desired.

SEE THAT THE DINING ROOM DOME LIGHT IS PLACED AT A PROPER HEIGHT. THE LAMPS SHOULD BE OUT OF THE LINE OF VISION

Indirect lighting example.

when introduced, a symbol of the freedom that electricity gave to the household. No more need the homeowner be constrained by the heavy forms of the gas pipes; the shower gave a sense of unrestrained license to the lighting.

After the gentle glow of gas fixtures, electricity at the turn of the century was seen as harsh and glaring. From about 1908, as a reaction to this, indirect and semi-direct lighting was introduced into the household. Bowls of opaque glass hung from the ceiling were used to avoid the directness of the harsh electric light, often left open at the top to provide reflective light off the lightly painted ceiling.

A Japonisme exterior light by Warren Hile.

THE MIDWEST

A BUILDING SHOULD APPEAR TO GROW easily from its site and be shaped to harmonize with its surroundings if nature is manifest there, and if not, try to make it as quiet, substantial, and organic as she would have been were the opportunity hers.

We of the Middle West are living on the prairie. The prairie has a beauty of its own and we should recognize and accentuate this natural beauty, its quiet level. Hence, gently sloping roofs, low proportions, quiet sky lines, suppressed heavy-set chimneys, and sheltering overhangs, low terraces, and out-reaching walls sequestering private gardens.

—FRANK LLOYD WRIGHT, *THE CAUSE OF ARCHITECTURE, I,* 1908

As with the Eastern Seaboard, the Arts and Crafts movement in the Midwest had many ties to England—from the early visits with lectures and exhibits by Walter Crane to C. R. Ashbee's several visits and lectures at Hull House, and from travels forth to England and the continent by the young architects and designers of the city to the founding of Hull House by Jane Addams and Ellen Gates Starr, under the direct influence of Ashbee's work at Toynbee Hall in London. But the direction of the movement in the Midwest, largely due to both the nature of Chicago and the direction given the movement by Frank Lloyd Wright, veered not only from its English origins but from the movement as it was unfolding elsewhere in the country.

"Chicago is the only American city I have seen where something absolutely distinctive in aesthetic handling of materials has been evolved out of the industrial system," C. R. Ashbee wrote during his second trip to America in 1901. Industrialism was the keynote of both the Midwest and the unique form of the

An original view of the dining room of the Frank Lloyd Wright home in Oak Park, Illinois.

Arts and Crafts movement that developed there. Chicago, destroyed in the fire started by Mrs. O'Leary's cow in 1871, proved fertile ground for new ideas as it rapidly rebuilt itself over the following two decades. Within years of the fire, the city's population had doubled, then doubled again as it built

The living room in Frank Lloyd Wright's home and studio located in Oak Park, Illinois. The color and the inglenook seats next to the fireplace are both original to the home. The horizontal sense is expressed and further strengthened by the wainscoting in olive green and wood strips that go around the room.

for itself the world's largest cable car system and the world's first skyscraper. Its newly developing culture was progressively inclined, and the businessmen of the city successfully fought for and won the right to hold the 1893 World's Colombian Exposition celebrating the 400th anniversary of the discovery of America.

In 1901, the same year that Ashbee visited the windy city, his friend, the already noted architect Frank Lloyd Wright, gave his celebrated lecture at Hull House, "The Art and Craft of the Machine," where he proclaimed, "…in the Machine lies the only future of art and craft—as I believe, a glorious future." Adaptation to the machine was at the core of the movement in the Midwest. Though there were many craftspeople in Chicago, St. Louis, Cincinnati, Milwaukee, and Minneapolis, the movement in

the Midwest was less about reverting to a distant past of medieval guilds and more about stepping forth into the new century with its vigorous progressivism as displayed by both the willingness to adopt to present-day technology and a new sense of design, which took its reference from the present rather than the past. In contrast to the message of Ruskin as passed down through Morris, Wright advocated in his polemical invocation "that the machine is capable of carrying to fruition high ideals in art—higher than the world has yet seen." It was in this adaptation to machine processes, in this clamoring rambunctiousness of progressive industrialism set against the peaceful, quiet horizontality of the prairie that allowed this style, which came to be called the Prairie School. It was a style that used clean, simple lines in an unornamented horizontal architecture and that encouraged a geometric clarity in both the furniture and window designs of the homes.

The Frank Lloyd Wright-designed spindle reclining chair and cantilevered couch as reproduced by Heinz and Company.

An exterior watercolor sketch of the Frank Lloyd Wright home painted by Wright himself. Having begun construction of his home before full development of his Prairie-style architecture, this building still retains the conventional look of the late-nineteenth-century shingle-style houses of the East Coast.

FUNCTION

IN THE BEGINNING, there was no thought of creating a new style, only a recognition of the fact that we should have in our homes something better suited to our needs and more expressive of our character as a people than *Gustav Stickley* imitations of the traditional styles, and a conviction that the best way to get something better was to go directly back to plain principles of construction and apply them to the making of simple, strong, comfortable furniture.—GUSTAV STICKLEY

Once the house is built, the walls are painted and stenciled, the woodwork polished, and the curtains hung, a house still needs life breathed into it—the life that can only come with the sound of a whistling tea kettle, a telephone ringing, and wind chimes tinkling in the backyard. It is the life that comes with the smell of Sunday dinner cooking, with hot showers taken on cold mornings, and with the hurried drinking of coffee while standing at the kitchen sink. And, it is the life that comes with the leisurely sinking back into a Morris chair, a fire snapping and crackling in the fireplace.

Function gives this life to our space. Where space,

A new Morris chair, as designed by Jaap Romijn and Friends, is a striking example of Romijn's subtle sense of proportion, learned through his boat-building experience in the Netherlands.

surface, and light give form to the home, function breathes the life into the body. It is about the way the house is used, about the chairs we sit upon and tables we eat on, about the beds we sleep in and the built-in bookshelves where we stack our copies of *The Craftsman*. It is about cooking in the kitchen and showering in the bathroom.

The furniture of the Arts and Crafts movement reflected not just the impact of a growing awareness of craft and a growing desire for a move towards the simple; it also reflected the changing needs and expectations of family life in the period. Settles, screens, and sideboards became standards for the home and the Morris chair became a veritable symbol of the period. Built-in bookshelves and china cabinets became expressive of the need for space conservation of the smaller houses of the simple life. Kitchens were designed for the first time for use without servants and became, as some from the era termed them, "factories for the little woman." Bathrooms not only showed the recent advances in plumbing, especially with the newfangled innovation of the shower, but having lately become an integral part of the home interior, as opposed to the outhouse, they became a decorative element, although it was the functionality that was emphasized in their decoration.

In this northern California house, note how the carpet defines the gathering area in front of the fireplace as the Morris chair anchors a corner area.

THE ELEMENTS OF DESIGN

After Joseph P. McHugh started production on his Mission-style furniture in the mid-1890s and Gustav Stickley launched his Craftsman "New Furniture" at the Grand Rapids Furniture Fair in 1900, other furniture companies were quick to switch their production lines to this popular modern style, to this simple, heavy, household furniture, made from quarter-sawn oak using sometimes-overexaggerated mortise-and-tenon joinery. It was, at the beginning, not an elegant furniture; it was more what one would expect to be made by a workman, a woodworker—simple, honest, and straightforward. These other companies used names such as Handcraft, Catskill Mission, or Oak-Worth to associate their lines with the Mission style in the public consciousness. They all marketed their lines not as comely pieces in themselves but promoted them as pieces integral to both the home and to the rediscovered sense of family. It was as though through this new, unpretentious simple design, through its overly emphasized craftsmanship, these pieces of furniture could define the values one held and could remind a person of the importance in life of the work of craft and its closeness to art.

Now, in these last two decades of the twentieth century, there has been a return to making the furniture of these turn-of-the-century companies. As the 1972 Princeton Arts and Crafts Movement in America exhibition revived interest in the Arts and Crafts object, the introduction in the spring of 1989 by the L. & J. G. Stickley Company of its Mission oak collection signaled the growing market demand for furniture, "in the style," of movement. Other large companies joined the parade, including the Lane Company and Richardson Brothers. Before the Stickley reintroduction of its Mission style, there had been craftspeople, such as David Berman of Trustworth and Tony Smith of Buffalo Studios, who had been making either reproductions or using elements from the Arts and Crafts in their crafts vocabulary. Then, suddenly, one could find a whole range of craftsmanship,

A new, removable-top Prairie table was crafted by Mack and Rodel, Cabinetmakers.

Through tenon with tusked wedge is the only ornamental feature of this Roycrofters' magazine pedestal except for the Roycroft symbol incised on the side. A Teco vase sits on the top shelf.

This visible treatment of mortise-and-tenon joinery is a confirmation of the craftsmanship. The diagonal angle of the ebony peg to the direction of the chair arm induces a lightness and playfulness. The Morris chair is by Berkeley Mills and Furniture.

A double-pegged tenon on a computer desk, adapted from a Harvey Ellis table design and designed and built by Brian Krueger.

from fine woodworkers working out of small shops or garages to the mass-produced, in-the-style-of, offerings of Crate & Barrel. Not only are Morris chairs, taborets, settles, screens, and spindle-backed dining chairs being produced for a public with a growing appetite, but one finds elements such as Charles Limbert cutouts, Greene & Greene cloud-lifts and splines, Roycroft tusked tenons, Stickley slats, Frank Lloyd Wright spindles, and Harvey Ellis inlays being added to coffee tables and chests of drawers to give them that "Arts and Crafts" look.

With the originally produced pieces still available, questions immediately arise: why should the newly produced furniture be purchased, and why is there such a market demand?

This detail is an example of a corbel on a Limbert table.

Without question, one of the most obvious reasons is the simple expedient of cost. When a period Morris chair costs a thousand dollars or more than its reproduced facsimile, or an original Harvey Ellis inlaid table costs a multitude of times more than its current-day reproduction, the tendency grows for the original high-end pieces to end up in private collections or museums instead of being used in people's homes.

Cost is still a consideration with pieces made today; not everyone can afford to hire an individual craftsperson to recreate an original Charles Rohlfs table for them. Individual craftsmanship, then as now, remains more for the well-to-do than the young homeowner. But, on the other hand, Gene Agress of the California company Berkeley Mills reminds his customers that he makes "a furniture that lasts a person his lifetime or more," and, therefore, they

Wood Classic's new spline design recalls the work of Greene and Greene.

must consider the relative cost.

Debey Zito, a San Francisco woodworker, advises her clients that to have a piece of furniture well built—a piece that will function and last for generations—is, in a sense, a way of preserving our scarce resources, a way of avoiding the need to purchase a cheaply made piece of furniture that will fall apart in a few years only to be replaced by another cheaply made piece of mass-produced furniture.

There is more than the issue of cost here, though. As was the impulse back then, there is a desire now to support craftsmanship, and the related desire to have the visible work of craftsmen expressed as part of one's life. These pronounced statements of craft—the mortise-and-tenon joinery, the tusked wedge, the corbels on the arms of chairs, the chamfered edge—were not new to the movement then, nor are they suddenly being rediscovered today. These basic elements of functional furniture structure have been and remain part of the craftsman's canon; what has changed is the public desire to display it openly in their homes, to

An exceptional bureau by a current craftsperson, Debey Zito. Note the detail in the handles.

From Wood Classics, a New Craftsman Morris chair with three adjustable back angles incorporates Chinese woodworking decorative elements such as those often seen in the work of Greene and Greene.

have it as an integral part of their lives. A key to understanding the furniture of the Arts and Crafts movement is to understand this need for visibility, if not overt exaggeration, of craftsmanship. Architectural historian Reyner Banham wrote that this was a movement with "an attitude in which the house becomes a shrine for objects of well-wrought functional art, and the inhabitants the devoted worshipers."

Even with all the large companies that are mass-producing pieces with "the look," there are still fine craftspeople who strive to replicate exact copies of the originals. Especially with the furniture of architects, like Frank Lloyd Wright, Greene and Greene, Purcell and Elmslie or George Washington Maher, who designed individual pieces for specific buildings, it is more than likely that original pieces have already found their way into the high-end collections or into museums making them inaccessible to the ordinary home. Jim Ipekjian, a Pasadena, California, craftsperson, reproduces the original designs of the work of the brothers Greene. To

A cherry easy chair by Debey Zito has a rabbit decorative cutout. Though stylistically adopting the Arts and Crafts designs, especially those of Greene and Greene, Zito defies using tropical wood cut from the rain forest, opting to use domestic lumber instead.

A new Morris chair by Berkeley Mills and Furniture displays bold assembly of massive, beautiful wood.

recreate a piece of their furniture, Ipekjian spends hours studying photographs, archival drawings, and if available, the actual piece, before he begins work on a new piece. The tools he works with are not so different, he is quick to point out, from those used by the Hall Brothers who milled and constructed the furniture designs of the Greenes. "One major difference is that in [the Halls' shop,] and it was probably common for most of the big production shops back then, they had a central power source with a shaft running through the floor and flat belts driving the individual saws. Now each machine has its own motor. That's different. But the saws today are streamlined a little bit. They may be a little bit more powerful. They're more efficient. but they're still saws."

THE MORRIS CHAIR

The Morris chair was first produced and sold by William Morris and Company in 1866. The company's business manager, George Warrington Taylor, had traveled the previous year to Sussex, where he had seen a chair in a carpenter's shop that had intrigued him. He sent a sketch of it to the Morris and Company resident architect, Philip Webb, who then refined the design for production. This original English version by Morris and Company, with its innovative element of a reclining back adjustable to various angles, was cushioned not only on the seat and back but on the arms as well and was lighter in weight than its American offspring. In 1902, after traveling to England, Gustav Stickley introduced into America his variation on this design. The Morris chair, as made by Stickley and most other producers of Mission furniture, became so widely used in all classes of homes and all areas of the country that a newspaper described the famous English poet-socialist-designer as "William Morris, of easy-chair fame."

The Stickley-introduced chair was heavier, more massive than its English forebear; it filled a room with a presence somewhat out of proportion to its function, but because of its stolid bulk, it served, like the fireplace and the hearth, as a kingpin to the other objects in the room. The historian Eileen Boris has written of how "the Morris chair stood for manly comfort" in the turn-of-the-century home, of how "many tastemakers recommended it for the den, the man's special room."

Usually, one found it nestled into the corner, angled to the straight lines of the walls, next to or near the fireplace, and almost always, a matching footstool was set in front of the chair for the man of the house to sit and rest his weary feet upon.

• *1. Four chairs constructed within the two-year period between 1906 and 1908 show how vast the permutations of Arts and Crafts design were. From left to right—the designs are by Charles Rennie Mackintosh, Greene and Greene, Frank Lloyd Wright, and Gustav Stickley.* • *2. A new cherry-wood chair by Debey Zito.* • *3. James Ipekjian of the James Randell Company built this exact copy of a Greene and Greene chair found in the Berkeley, California, Thorsen House.*

This spindle Morris chair is currently being made by L. & J. G. Stickley Company.

SIGNATURES OF THE MAKERS

1. CHARLES LIMBERT (1854-1923)

Influenced from Charles Rennie Mackintosh and the Vienna Viener Werkstatte, Charles Limbert produced furniture that was distinguished by what A. Patricia Bartinique has called his "Slab-and-Cut-Out-Designs," that is, furniture constructed of broad planks of wood with decorative cutouts reminiscent of the European Arts and Crafts.

2. THE SHOP OF THE CRAFTERS AT CINCINNATI (1904-1920)

Decorated with colored inlay work, Oscar Onken (1858-1948) attempted to integrate the decorative designs of the European Arts and Crafts designs with the visually simple lines of the American Mission furniture.

3. GREENE & GREENE

Designed for placement in particular spots in houses of their design, the furniture of the Charles (1868-1957) and Henry (1870-1954) Greene displays both a visual and actual level of craftsmanship almost out of touch with the rest of the movement. The work of their high period was distinguished by gentle curves in the arms and backs of their chairs, inlay using mother-of-pearl, fruitwood, pewter and copper; "dancing pegs" and splines made of ebony; and the "Cloud Lift," the gentle rise they used on the backs and rungs of their chairs and on the handles of their cabinets. There was in their work an overall sense of design which referred back to the Orient, to Chinese furniture design and Japanese motifs. As Charles Ashbee wrote in admiration about Charles Greene after meeting him, "The spell of Japan is upon him…."

4. FRANK LLOYD WRIGHT (1867-1959)

As with other architect-designed furniture, rather than designing pieces for production, Wright designed furniture that was individually designed for his clients and intended to be placed in one particular spot in one particular home. His pieces have a heaviness about them, a sense of being rooted to their location. Wright's furniture was noted for being designed not just to serve a function but more to define the architectural space of the room.

5. GUSTAV STICKLEY (1857-1942)

Using quarter-sawn oak finished with fumed ammonia, Stickley produced furniture that epitomized the belief that the construction should dictate the design. The mortise-and-tenon joinery, the heavy emphasis upon the hardware, the simple squared pulls, all emphasized that this was a furniture meant for a new lifestyle. In 1903, Stickley hired the architect-designer-artist Harvey Ellis (1852-1904), who brought a lighter, more graceful touch to the furniture designs by use of arched aprons and overhanging tops. The keyed tenon joints were eliminated and decorative inlays of conventionalized floral motifs made with copper, pewter and wood were added to the furniture.

6. CHARLES ROHLFS (1853-1936)

Overtly medieval with touches of Art Nouveau, the furniture of Rohlfs was heavy, carved, and ornamented with conventionalized motifs.

7. THE ROYCROFTERS (1856-1915)

Elbert Hubbard began producing furniture for use on his Roycroft Campus as early as 1896 and began offering it through mail order in 1901. Marked with his Roycroft R symbol, with exaggerated details, tusked tenons, the pieces were uniformly heavy and simple.

8. THE FURNITURE SHOP (1906-1920)

The artist-designers Arthur (1860-1945) and Lucia (1870-1955) Mathews formed The Furniture Shop in 1906 to meet the demand created by the destructiveness of the San Francisco Earthquake for furnishings and fixtures of the wealthy San Franciscans. Though much of the production of the shop was geared towards commercial, unornamented work, a significant amount was decorated with handcarved and painted ornamentation.

SETTLES, SCREENS, AND SIDEBOARDS

With the new openness and changed functionality of the houses of the Arts and Crafts era, new needs of furniture, exemplified by settles, screens, and sideboards, were necessary.

The word *settle,* when used as a noun and not a verb, was like many of the references of the Arts and Crafts movement, a throwback to the twelfth century, this time referring to a wooden bench with arms and a high solid back with storage under the seat. In the Arts and Crafts vocabulary, it was used to refer to what shortly before would have been called a "sofa." With its high arms and rectilinear box shape, it served to define the space into which it was placed. In a room, it could form a divider; in front of a fireplace, it formed a private space. The screen,

Inspired by the work of Greene and Greene, the craftsman David Hellman built this living-room set.

A settle in the living room of one of the original Craftsman homes, number 104, built in 1911 in New Jersey.

another definer of space, was a throwback to not just the medieval but to the simple, furniture-free existence of the Japanese room that had been introduced at the 1876 centennial exposition in Philadelphia. In the bedroom, it formed a dressing area; in the living room or library, it created an intimate area or divided a room. With the simplification of the home and the absence

Eschewing the comfort of the padded backs and arms of the Victorian sofa, a settle not only gave reference back to the medieval bench, it was also more compatible with the newfound desire for a more simple life.

An original Craftsman screen backs a Dirk van Erp lamp and a cushioned L. & J. G. Stickley settle.

This Gustav Stickley sideboard has been placed, as it was meant to be, in a dining room.

of servants, the sideboard as a staging area for the meal came to replace not just the servant but the pantry. It served to hold silver and china, place mats and tablecloths, and in a way, came to represent in the dining room what the Hoosier cabinet represented in the kitchen, a way that the housewife could manage her home in this new age of functionality.

CRAFTSMAN CLOCKS

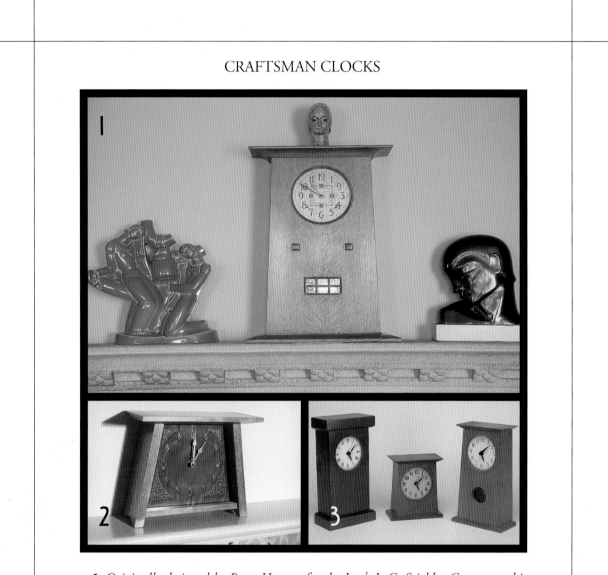

• **1.** *Originally designed by Peter Hansen for the L. & J. G. Stickley Company, this mantel clock has been reissued by the Stickley Company as part of their Mission Oak Collection.* • **2.** *This mantel clock was crafted by Drake Adkinsson of AKA Drake Custom Furniture.* • **3.** *Three mantel clocks by Paul Kemner Furniture Craftsman, who has been inspired by Gustav Stickley's woodworking ideal of using good quality, quarter-sawn white oak. Kemner uses the same ammonia-fuming technique on his wood and carefully applies shellac and wax.*

Above: Another example of adaptation.

Right: Turn-of-the-century design does not always meet our end-of-the-century needs. Here, in a northern California bungalow, Craftsman elements have been adapted to modern usage.

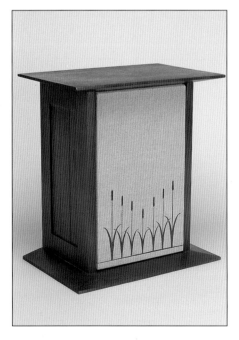

Paul Kemner Furniture Craftman designed this contemporary stereo speaker done in the Arts and Crafts-style with "cattail" stencils on natural linen grill cloth.

NEW USES OF OLD FORMS

As a good deal of the design of the furniture then was a reaction to the changed needs of the household, so today too this is a reality. At the turn of the century, it was a new and innovative thing for Gustav Stickley to design a telephone stand for the home. Today one needs furniture to hold stereo and CDs and to fit a computer. One looks today for entertainment centers instead of bookcases, for coffee tables instead of library tables, and these are needs which cannot be met by purchasing furniture of the period.

THE MACHINE & THE AMATEUR

JOHN RUSKIN, IN HIS ONGOING BATTLE against industry and in support of the laborer, declared bluntly and simply that "machine work is bad, it is dishonest." In his Ruskin-influenced turn away from machine produced goods and towards handmade craft items, William Morris came head-to-head with the basic paradox of the movement: that either one adapts one's craft to modern means of production, with the resulting loss of the "craftsman's joy in his labor," or one produces individual pieces of such price so as to turn them into trinkets for the wealthy. Craft was a product of a time before capitalism, which in part explains its attractiveness to those who became disenchanted with the harsh results of the capitalistic industrial system. So craft and craftsmanship came to represent much more than the mere production of an object; tethered to that object was an alternative vision to what work, the work place, and man's joy in his work could be all about. Morris, faced with this paradox, gave up and turned to socialism, declaring what has become a rallying cry for the movement: "What business have we with art at all, unless all can share it?"

From the making of copper candle shades to denim portiere, women busied themselves decorating their home sanctuaries with their handicrafts. With much attention given today to famed designers of the Arts and Crafts movement, the do-it-yourself spirit that resided in the movement tends to be overlooked.

The movement in America rarely took this near-Luddite view of the machine; on the contrary, much of what was produced here was machine made despite all the publicity around handmaking and handcrafting the work. Elbert Hubbard was probably the most famous of the mystifiers, declaring in his 1904 catalog that the Roycroft furniture was "handmade from start to finish," and in the catalog of a year later, writing that "Roycroft furniture is all made in a

cabinet shop; we do not have a furniture factory." He was also apt to avow that each piece of furniture was signed by the man who made it, though this, too, was untrue. Gustav Stickley was more honest in his appraisal of the need for machinery, justifying his factory by writing that "given the real need for production and the fundamental desire for self expression, the machine can be put to all its legitimate uses as an aid to, and preparation for, the work of the hand, and the result be quite as vital and satisfying as the best work of the hand done." Ernest Batchelder put it more succinctly when he wrote that "the evil of machinery is largely a question of whether machinery shall use men or men shall use machinery." So in America, it was not the use of machinery that was questioned, it was rather how it was to be used and, resultingly, how the workplace was to be affected by its use. As Robert Edwards has written, "At the core of Arts and Crafts philosophy lay the concept that work should be the creative and joyful essence of daily life rather than the mere act of sustenance."

There arose a certain amount of craft work outside of the factory, which was intended to be part of this creative and joyful essence of daily life—this was the craft work of amateurs. Hand work in one's home, in the evenings after work or on weekends, was encouraged by much of the popular literature of the day. *Popular Mechanics* published a series of handbooks how to make Mission furniture and Mission lamps, providing dia-

Sue Mack assembles a piece of furniture at the Mack and Rodel woodshop in Maine.

Michael Adams, well known for his van Erp-style lamps, works metal at his Aurora Studios in Oswego, New York.

grams, materials lists, and practical tips for construction. *The Ladies' Home Journal, House Beautiful,* and *Home and Garden* all had articles on the handmaking of home furnishings by the housewife and furniture by her husband, on everything from stenciling curtains to the making of a freestanding three-panel screen and from hand-tooling leather purses to the use of pyrography, a method of burning wood to give a decorative aged look. Stickley's *The Craftsman* especially promoted this idea of the talented amateur, a promotion that brought a certain backlash because those who made their livelihood by craft began to complain about the poor quality and lowering of standards of the craft being produced by the amateurs.

The end result was that the machine, as Frank Lloyd Wright averred, "by its wonderful shaping, smoothing, and repetitive capacity, has made it possible to so use it without waste that the poor as well as the rich may enjoy today beautiful surface treatments of clean strong forms." With the acceptance of the machine, products could be produced that need not be reserved for the well-to-do alone; it enabled the movement to become something capable of stirring the middle classes—though for it to be more than just a style, more than production of symbols and totems of a better life, these middle classes needed, as many did, to adopt the making of these objects into their lives.

Though Berkeley Mills and Furniture in Berkeley, California, is a production shop, each piece of furniture is milled, constructed, and finished by one individual craftsperson.

COMMUNITY

A HOME MUST BE CONSIDERED not only from the personal standpoint, but also in relation to the community; and since a home once built must stand for many years, much thought should be given to the building to make it one that will add to the beauty of the neighborhood.

—MABEL TUKE PRIESTMAN, *ARTISTIC HOMES*

The Roycroft Chapel, built in 1899, is today used as the East Aurora Town Hall, New York.

Close-up view of the Roycroft Chapel.

The idea of community is intrinsic to the Arts and Crafts impulse. In 1871, John Ruskin formed the first utopian crafts community with his Guild of St. George, long before the phrase "Arts and Crafts" had ever been applied to the movement. In his romantic rebellion against industrialized mass production, Ruskin strove for a simple lifestyle in his guild, one healthy for both hands and minds, and based upon what he called his "new feudalism." The guild served as inspiration for crafts guilds and communities in both England and America in the years that followed. In England, there was Charles Ashbee's Guild of Handicraft; in America, the utopian visions ranged from Beaux Arts Village on Puget Sound near Seattle to the single-tax community of Arden, which survives to this day, to Will Price's Rose Valley Commu-

nity in Pennsylvania and Ralph Radcliffe Whitehead's Byrdcliffe Art Colony in upstate New York. Inherent in all of these communities was the idea of gathering crafts-people in mutually supportive societies, away from urban blight, where they might perform their skilled artsmanship, not as "cogwheels," as Ruskin warned, but as handcrafters able to value the roughness and individuality inherent in handmade craft and be able to do their art, which Ruskin defined as "man's expression of his joy in labour."

The idea of community was inherent also in the building of houses associated with the movement. With the almost overpowering strength of style certain architects brought to their work, gatherings of their homes were formed that did more than just form groupings of homes by a specific architect; simply through their congregation, these clusters of houses created a community of harmony, making more of the whole than of the sum of their individual parts. In Pasadena, the gathering above the Arroyo of wooden Japonisme-style homes was built by Greene and Greene. Connected by the train line to Chicago's center is the community of Oak Park, where Frank Lloyd Wright built not only his own home and studio and the homes of many of his clients but, as one wanders the verdant grid of the neighborhood, one finds a whole bevy of houses built by those of the Prairie School who were so influenced by Wright.

After the turn of the century, this clustering of like homes happened on a grander scale with the less-grand houses that came to be called bungalows. These low-cost, middle-class dwellings of single story for the simple life covered whole blocks of cities as they expanded outward, often leading into the suburbs with the ever-increasing tentacles of the train and trolley-car lines. Bungalows not only provided housing for the up-and-coming middle class, but they gave the middle classes a sense of the countryside while allowing them to remain tied to their jobs in the city. In general, bungalows were built not by the block but rather in twos and threes by individual carpenters. They worked from plans bought for a few dollars from bungalow magazines or plan books, such as the 1911 *Radford's Artistic Bungalows* or, on the West Coast, Henry Wilson's *Bungalow Magazine*. These publications did much more than just sell the bungalow, though that they did well; as part of their sales pitch, they advocated a whole style of life that revolved around the bungalow with its little yard and rose garden, a style of life centered around the fireplace—"the heart of the home"—the family, and the return to a more simple way of life.

Houses could also be bought by mail and shipped to a newly purchased lot, ready to construct—all the parts and pieces, down to the last screw, freighted to the job site in crates, ready to be unpacked and put together like a Chinese block puzzle. Most of the companies supplying homes by mail were centered in the Midwest because of the availability of lumber and lumber mills. After the first decade of the century, companies such as the Gordon Van Tine Company; Aladdin; E. F. Hodgson Company; Sears, Roebuck, and Company; and their arch rival Montgomery Ward, began offering anything from a "knock-down summer cottage" to two-story houses complete with lighting, heating and plumbing systems, wallpaper, and furniture.

ROSE VALLEY AND BYRDCLIFFE

What is domestic architecture? Not pictures of houses, but houses. Not transplanted and unrelated diagrams, but stone and brick, wood, iron and glass, built up into an expressive envelope for human desires and sentiments.
            —THE CRAFTSMAN, 1909, WILLIAM PRICE

Today, upon entering Rose Valley outside Philadelphia, one cannot help but notice the sudden serenity that takes over the senses, the feeling of stepping back in time and enjoying the quietude of the vista along Ridley Creek while wandering past the buildings of rustic timbers, Moravian tiles, stucco, and stone. At the end of a narrow roadway are the two old textile mills where, in 1901, William Lightfoot Price, the prominent Philadelphia architect, decided to start his Rose Valley Furniture Shops, the first of the projected crafts shops that were to form the heart of the Rose Valley Association he was organizing. The concept for the association was for artisans to gather together in the valley to work under the

Gateposts in Rose Valley, designed by Will Price and inset with Mercer tiles, are placed in many entrances to streets and lanes.

appellation of The Rose Valley Shops, producing "structures, articles, materials, and products involving artistic handicraft." The association acted as landlord and granted a literal seal of approval to the craft work. Those who were qualified to rent space and work in the valley were allowed to use the Rose Valley seal on their products and sell their work under the auspices of the association in Philadelphia. In those first few years of the association, books, metalwork, and pottery, as well as Price's furniture, were all produced in the valley. By 1903 Horace Traubel, Walt Whitman's biographer, was publishing *The Artsman* as "the mouthpiece of Rose Valley," even though it was published and printed in Philadelphia.

The community, like most communities of the day, was not a financial success. The pottery was discontinued by 1905, the furniture shop lasting only a year longer. *The Artsman* ceased publication by 1907. While the Rose Valley Association did not last out the decade, another allied organization, The Rose Valley Folk, did. The Association was for crafts and craftspeople; the Folk was organized for dealing with the nuts and bolts of communal living and lasted through the 1920s. The Guild Hall—today, Hedgerow Theater, where the Folk met and where

Thunderbird Lodge was converted from an old barn made of stone that was remodeled by Will Price in 1904.

events, concerts, plays, and musicals were organized—has remained to this day an active part of the community.

Although not long-lived as a crafts community, the achievements of Rose Valley were recognized widely by others in the Arts and Crafts movement. In her *History of the Arts and Crafts Movement in America,* Mabel Tuke Priestman compared it favorably with C. R. Ashbee's Guild of Handicraft, and Ashbee himself particularly praised Will Price's mastery of the vernacular architectural vocabulary, describing in his writings that Price "has like most of us who have studied the arts and crafts and feel the humanity underlying the movement, the conviction that if the movement is to find itself, it must speak in a voice of its own...."

A year after the beginning of Rose Valley, the wealthy Englishman Ralph Radcliffe Whitehead founded his Arts and Crafts community in upstate New York, which he called Byrdcliffe, using a compound of his and his wife's, Jane Byrd McCall's, middle names. Whitehead had studied under John Ruskin at Oxford as a young man and later, forming a friendship with the great man, traveled with him to Venice. He moved to America in 1890, marrying Jane McCall, a wealthy Philadelphia socialite, two years later. Together they traveled west to Santa Barbara, where they built an Italianate villa on an estate they called Arcady. There, in cottages and studios, they encouraged young artists, craftspeople, and musicians to visit and work. Through this precursor of Byrdcliffe, Whitehead met the two people who were to help him establish his arts colony in New York: the poet and novelist Hervey White and the head of the Stanford Art Department, Bolton Brown.

With Brown and White's help, Whitehead began buying up land in the Woodstock valley on the south side of Overlook Mountain. It was said that he spent a half million dollars buying the fifteen hundred acres and building the thirty buildings that formed the colony. He bought all the equipment needed for crafts production and installed baths and toilets in all the cottages, an unusual feature in that day and age. Automobiles and electricity were not allowed in until the 1920s.

During its heyday as a summer arts colony, craftspeople at Byrdcliffe produced furniture, metalwork, weaving, and pottery; they had musical evenings and an active theater. Dances were held twice a week in the art studio as well as on the grassy terrace of the Whitehead home, White Pines, where Jane Whitehead, dressed in flowing white, would lead the others in "Morris dancing."

Like the Rose Valley furniture, much of the Byrdcliffe furniture was built by cabinetmakers and woodworkers who belonged to the Society of Arts and Crafts in Boston and was heavy in construction and too costly for the average middle-class homemaker. Local woods such as poplar and oak were used in the making of the furniture, reflecting Ruskin's belief of using indigenous sources and

A Rose Valley home designed by Will Price incorporates Mercer tiles set into the plaster of the exterior walls.

Ralph Whitehead named his home White Pines, not just as another variation upon his name nor so much for the trees that stood beside it but more because the name reminded him of White Nights, the name of an Umbrian farm written about in one of his favorite books, Marius.

materials for crafts. The furniture making, which Whitehead had hoped would be the financial mainstay of the community, ceased production by 1905, and Whitehead himself turned to weaving. When Bolton Brown and Hervey White both ended up at odds with Whitehead and were asked to leave the colony, they both stayed in Woodstock, Brown teaching art and White writing, eventually publishing the literary magazine *The Wild Hawk.*

The arts colony ended as more a summertime family retreat and boarding house for the Whitehead family, though they tried through their own private funding to keep it in the spirit of the arts and crafts by providing a summertime site for craftspeople to work. Whitehead died in 1929, Jane in 1955. When their son, Peter Whitehead, who had continued the tradition of encouraging craftspeople and artists to live at Byrdcliffe, died in 1975, he deeded Byrdcliffe to the Woodstock Guild of Craftsmen. It remains an active colony of artisans and artists to this day.

In the tradition of William Morris, Ralph Whitehead added his Loom Room to White Pines, connected to the main house by a covered bridge, and set up spinning wheels, looms, and dye pots where he would work with others at weaving.

At Byrdcliffe, natural burlap was stretched over the walls of the living hall of Ralph Whitehead's home, and the woodwork was stained a transparent blue green. Henry Chapman Mercer had his Moravian Pottery and Tile Works provide Whitehead with a specifically designed green tile to set in around the fireplace. A table and chairs made at the Byrdcliffe furniture shop are in front of the fireplace.

THE WEST

"ONE THING NOTICEABLE ABOUT A CALIFORNIA HOME is its hominess. How many houses one may see that are pretty or original, often costly and elaborate, filled to overflowing with rare things beautiful in themselves but after all it is the homelike house that one's heart goes out to. The one with its open fire and cozy chair and a hundred other little things that help to make life easy. But it takes thought and experience and great pains to plan something that one does not tire of."

—CHARLES GREENE, *HOME MAKING IN CALIFORNIA*, 1907

The courtyard of the Duncan-Irwin House, taken from the Katherine Duncan House, was built overlooking the Arroyo Seco in Pasadena. In 1906, the Greene brothers altered it so dramatically for its new owner, Theodore Irwin, that it was transfigured into one of the most masterful adaptations of Japanese-influenced architecture in America.

The East carried the Arts and Crafts movement from England, and the Midwest made it into something truly American, but the isolated West was able to achieve a freedom and newness with the movement that could only have come from its detachedness. Separated from the rest of the country by the great wall of mountains, there was a feeling of new beginnings along the Pacific coast, a sense of rebirth in the land for the emigrants and tourists who traveled from the East. Glorified as a land of sunshine and a paradise where the sky was blue 365 days a year, it drew upon a population arriving often for reasons of health but always with dreams of a new life away from the rigidity and stolidness of the lands to the east.

In both a literal and a figurative way, the West was closer to the other East, to Asia, than it was to the rest of

The Roy Lanterman House, named El Retiro, built in 1915 from the designs provided by the architecture of Arthur Haley, was designed for the mildness of the southern Californian climate to include sleeping and wide porches.

Built high on a hill overlooking Los Angeles, Hollyhock House was designed by Frank Lloyd Wright in 1905 for Aline Barnsdall. Barnsdall's favorite flower, the hollyhock, provided Wright's design inspiration for the abstract decorative patterns in the concrete ornamentation, the art-glass windows, and the oak furniture.

Irving Gill's McMakin House is expressive of Gill's quest for simplicity and regionalism in architectural design.

the country. One found this sense of Asia coupled with the new freedom of the West most evident in the work of the two brothers Charles and Henry Greene, who produced an exquisite body of work, primarily in Pasadena, California. As the English Arts and Crafts advocate C. R. Ashbee wrote about Charles Greene, the older of the Greene brothers who did the majority of the designing, "The spell of Japan is on him, he feels the beauty and makes magic out of the horizontal line." The architecture of the Greenes is noted for its adaptation to the mild climate of southern California, for the way it used spacious open sleeping porches and the overhanging wide roofs with extended eaves to expand outward the

boundaries of the house.

At the southern tip of California was perhaps the purest expression of the Arts and Crafts movement, the work of Irving Gill. Totally eschewing all ornamentation, working with bold squares and arches, flat planes and straight lines, broken only by a bougainvillea or creeping ivy, Gill designed homes as variants upon the cube, perfectly sited for both the immediate landscape and the region. As he wrote in a late issue of *The Craftsman*, "There is something very restful and satisfying to my mind in the simple cube house with creamy walls, sheer and plain, rising boldly into the sky, unrelieved by cornices or overhang of roof, unornamented save for the

The George W. Marston House in San Diego was built by Irving Gill and William Hebbard in 1904.

vines that soften a line or creepers that wreathe a pillar or flowers that inlay color more sentiently than any tile could do."

Oddly, though much of the northern California activity of the Arts and Crafts movement took place within San Francisco, the style of home that came to be identified with the movement in the north developed across the bay in Berkeley. The house that Bernard Maybeck designed for his friend Charles Keeler in 1894 and the subsequent formation in 1898 of the Hillside Club by the two men set the tone not only for what is now known as the Bay Area-style of architecture but further established an environmental and community awareness that has lasted through to this day. Under the guidance of Keeler and Maybeck, as the landscape histo-

The frieze in the Lanterman House billiard room has been carefully restored by the firm of Pinson and Ware.

In the upstairs room of the Charles Keeler Studio, the simple wood-paneled walls, the carved-beam ceilings, and the built-in bookcases exemplify both a way of life and the style of architecture in the northern California turn-of-the-century home.

rian David Streatfield has written, "Roads were treated as country lanes, following the contours of the hills and avoiding existing trees and rock outcrops. The blocks of houses were irregular in shape, with individual houses stepped back into the slope to minimize disturbance of the site." The houses that came to cover the Berkeley hills, many of them built by Maybeck, were statements in redwood of the simple life, open to nature, often with references to either the medieval or the Japonisme, built with the community in mind.

ALLUSION

"GOOD GRACIOUS!' REPLIED MR. MORRIS, 'what is there in modern life for the man who seeks beauty?' Nothing—you know it quite well.…The age is ugly—to find anything beautiful we must 'look before and after.' Of course, if you don't want to make it beautiful, you may deal with modern incident, but you will get a mere statement of fact—that is science.…No, if a man nowadays wants to do anything beautiful he must just choose the epoch which suits him and identify himself with that—he must be a thirteenth-century man, for instance."

William Morris (1834–1896)

—FROM "ART, CRAFT, AND LIFE. A CHAT WITH MR. WILLIAM MORRIS," *THE DAILY CHRONICLE,* 1893

Allusion is the way homeowners give their homes meaning by surrounding themselves with symbols that have association for them—the references and reminders of their pasts that they incorporate into their living space. Motif and design become metaphors for that which we hold valuable. In the final outcome, it is allusion that most significantly demonstrates what the Arts and Crafts home is all about. Allusion is within the structure, the interior, and the objects placed inside; in the colors we choose, the motifs we stencil; in the ruggedness of wall texture or the sheerness of curtain fabric where we discover the references and ideas that

The library of the George Marston House in San Diego holds many direct references to the Arts and Crafts movement—from the Navajo rugs on the Gustav Stickley library table and the Stickley Brothers round table to the Old Mission Kopper Kraft bookends and humidor on the library table to the small matte-green jardinère on the window sill. Today open to the public, the Marston House was designed in 1904 by Irving Gill and William S. Hebbard for the owner of Marston's Department Store, local distributors of Stickley's United Crafts furniture and furnishing.

the movement is all about.

The exterior use of logs, clinker bricks, and fieldstones give the home reference to the region and to the idea of nature. The colors home-owners paint the walls are a reference back to the outdoors, to the green of spring or the golden rust of autumn leaves. A conventionalized flower pattern on the wallpaper provides a reminder of the flora outside. The hand-hammered copper of a Dirk van Erp lamp retains a memory of the craftsman's rhythmic hammering. The Japonisme-style vision of The Gamble House of Greene and Greene, the Southwest Indian characteristics of Charles Lummis's El Alisal, or the medievalism of Henry Chapman Mercer's Fonthill—all allude to the simple life and ideals of preindustrial, crafts-based societies.

The smaller brown vase was made by Pigsah Forest; the tea tile and the larger vase with the blue, high-glaze finish were made by California Faience.

One of the ideas of the Arts and Crafts movement was that craft work could be therapeutic for the ills created by the industrialized society. The vases on this Gustav Stickley three-drawer server are by potteries that were begun to provide therapy for convalescing patients. The tallest vase is by Arequipa Pottery, a California pottery. The other vases are from Marblehead Pottery in Massachusetts. The two small dishes are works of Gertrude and Otto Natzler, and the lamp with a red warty finish, is by Dirk van Erp. The painting is by Marion Holden Pope.

CERAMIC WORKS

One day in the spring of 1897, the self-taught archeologist Henry Chapman Mercer was looking for a pair of tongs for his old-fashioned fireplace by picking through, as his biographer Cleota Reed has written, "a disordered pile of old wagons, gum-tree salt boxes, flax-brakes, straw beehives, tin dinner-horns, rope-machines, and spinning-wheels." This picking led him to the realization that what was in front, if he looked from a new point of view, was the entire history of the area. Over the three decades of his life, he gathered a massive collection of "tools," as he called them, the implements of crafts that "would illustrate the daily life of a people at a given time," the time that was being illustrated was an America before the industrial revolution, a time when craft was still a part of people's lives.

Mercer's interest in preserving these objects grew to a concern for preserving the actual crafts processes; specifically he became interested in the potteries that produced the traditional Pennsylvania-German redware. At one time, the area of Pennsylvania where he lived was dotted with these potteries, but by the time he became aware of them, there were only three left. He spent a short time working with one of the potters, and then, in 1898, founded his own pottery, the Moravian Pottery and Tile Works. He had already been inducted into the Arts and Crafts ethos as a student of Harvard while studying

Framing the windows, Charles Lummis used his own glass photographic negatives to create an effect much like stained glass.

under Charles Elliot Norton, a close friend of Ruskin and contemporary of Morris, so when he began production of his tiles, not only were they handmade but the first motifs he chose were from the medieval, specifically from ancient tiles discovered in English abbeys and from medieval English paving tiles.

Because Mercer's tiles were hand fabricated, they were irregular in shape and surface—a detail that caused frustration with architects and contractors, who were used to the precise dimensions of machine-made tiles. At times, he sent his own tile setter to work with builders so they could work out and understand the subtle beauty in the uneven floor surfaces created with his tiles. "The work had become a missionary one," Mercer asserted. "I have been compelled to teach architects and decorators to

On the wall above the L. & J. G. Stickley Company entertainment center is a gouache and India-ink painting, entitled Ginkgo Twig, *done by Anita Munman in the style of Hannah Borger Overbeck, one of the four sisters who founded Overbeck Pottery in Indiana. The Morris chair and side table are also by Stickley Company, and the lamp is by Mica Lamp Company.*

think as much of my product as I think of it."

Mercer's tiles became widely used in work of the Arts and Crafts period. Ralph Adams Cram and Bertram Goodhue used his tile in the churches they designed. Will Price used them extensively in his architecture, especially in Rose Valley outside of Philadelphia, using them as ornamental accents in the rough-cast stucco exteriors.

What Mercer started was continued by others, such as Grueby Faience of Boston and Pewabic Pottery in Detroit—both lines of tile under the influence of the

A Dirk van Erp lamp paired with a California Faience vase.

Matte green was a favorite color for Arts and Crafts pottery. From left to right, a hand-thrown vase by Matt Carlton from the Bauer Pottery, a California Faience bowl, and a Princess vase from the Bauer Pottery.

Moravian work. On the West Coast, Ernest Batchelder, a noted teacher of design, put theory into practice when, in 1909, inspired by a batch of Moravian tiles he had ordered to show his students, he built a studio in the backyard of his home and started making low-relief, hand-pressed tiles similar to those produced by Mercer. The tiles he had ordered for classroom use ended up being used to decorate the chimney and fireplace of his home. With the rapid growth of southern California, it was an opportune time to begin a tile business, and twice Batchelder had to move his studio to handle the growth. His tiles could often be seen in the fireplaces and hearth, in kitchens or bathrooms, or along the walkways of the bungalows being so rapidly built not just in California but across the nation.

An earlier example from the Rookwood Pottery shows the clear Japanese influence it the asymmetrical design on the floral motif.

Hand-pressed tilework to go around a fireplace is by Mary Glass-Tapp of Tile Restoration Center, who works today in the tradition of the famous Arts and Crafts tile maker Ernest Batchelder. Batchelder, a well-known designer and educator, began making tiles with his students in his backyard while he finished building his bungalow that over-looks the wooded Arroyo in Pasadena.

A "Peacock" tile by Tile Restoration Center is a reproduction of an Ernest Batchelder design.

Next to the clock are three pieces of metalwork from the Heinz Art Metal Shop. The silver overlays are bonded to the bronze surface by a heating method called "sintering."

In 1910, a writer in *House and Garden* wrote of a visit to "the art rooms of a famous dealer," where she examined a number of vases and considered their domestic uses. One vase she admired was "…honest, artistic, a rough green surface…just the setting needed to bring out the beauty of blossom and branch." A Native American jar she imagined filled with goldenrod; and of the beauty of "a large jar, the shape simple and graceful," she writes, "it would have been a sacrilege to lessen by placing therein distracting flower and leaf."

Not all vases were meant to hold objects; not uncommonly they were designed to be admired as works in themselves, held to the same rank as a painting on the wall. Their function comes both from their balancing and carrying forth of other patterns and colors in the room and from images, a conventional leaf or a medieval motif, which hold meaning for the person who places the vase in its location.

Pottery was an ideal expression of the Arts and Crafts movement. It comprised individual craftsmanship that could be done on a small scale; it was an everyday item that had household use; it was tied to the region and the land by its use of material; and, most

Irving Gill's ingenuity in the care and economy of home design produced this interior window that opens into an otherwise dark closet, adding to the charm and beauty of this home.

In the end, the goal of any interior is to provide a warm, comfortable space for living, surrounded by loved objects. Here in this home is a Morris chair, footstool, and side table by Warren Hile. The lamp is a modern reproduction by Mica Lamps.

importantly, it demanded a close allegiance between the potter and the decorator—that is, the crafter and the designer. Indeed, at many of the potteries, this division was one of gender—the men threw the pots and the women decorated them. But the important point was that, for the most part, this was a time of handwork, of hand-thrown pots with hand-done glazes and impressions being incised, pressed, or painted onto the surfaces. Earliest of these art potteries was the pioneering work of the heiress Maria Longworth Nichols and her Rookwood Pottery in Cincinnati, which Chicago Arts and Crafts advocate Oscar Lovell Triggs called the ideal workshop. "It is, in a

A fireplace decorated with Rookwood high-glaze tiles.

The Rookwood Pottery in Cincinnati, Ohio, opened in 1880 and headed by artist Maria Longworth Nichols (1849–1932), became the most successful art pottery in America, using a variety of styles, shapes, colors, and techniques.

A fireplace with Grueby tiles in a custom Stickley-built home. In addition to these plain tiles, Grueby produced more decorative tiles with fauna and flora such as iris, tulip, water lily, pine trees, ships, and pastoral imagery.

"Nocturne," a wood-block print by William S. Rice. Rice was introduced to Japanese color prints at the 1915 Panama Pacific Exposition in San Francisco.

sense," he wrote, "a school of handicraft, an industrial art museum, and a social center." Many of those who worked at Rookwood went on to found their own potteries. For example, Artus van Briggle, after three years' sponsored training in Paris, returned inspired by the French Art Nouveau movement and, in ill health, moved to Colorado to do his own work, emphasizing the romantic lyrical Art Nouveau shapes rather than surface decorations.

It was a matter of pride for William Henry Grueby that each piece of the pottery from his company was shaped on a potter's wheel and decorated by young women. His pottery, and especially his famous matte green glaze—"its color is the suggestion of the deepest

Above: Original Prairie School lighting provides even light for this bathroom. The bathroom hardware was hand hammered by Tony Smith of Buffalo Studios.

Right: A hanging wall sconce designed by Greene and Greene for the Gamble House in Pasadena.

Left: Set into a concrete wall at the Moravian Pottery and Tile Works, an embedded tile depicts the ideal of preindustrial craftsmanship.

green of a very dark melon"—was championed by Gustav Stickley, who not only shared exhibit space with him but used Grueby vases in typical Craftsman room settings for *The Craftsman.* Grueby vases "captured precisely the quiet mood sought," Stickley wrote.

In 1909, the grandson of the Fulper Pottery Company founder introduced a line of decorative ceramics called Vasekraft, which included not just decorative items such as vases and jardinières but utilitarian household items such as candleholders, lamps, bookends, and bowls. Though a number of potteries, including Rookwood, Newcomb College, Teco, and Grueby, produced bases for lamps, only Fulper produced both a base and an accompanying shade.

Not all pieces of the pottery of the Arts and Crafts movement were handthrown. Some ceramic lines, such as the Teco Ware of the Gated Pottery, produced work that came out of molds. The designs for Teco pieces, often done by well-known architects in nearby Chicago,

including Frank Lloyd Wright, were of geometric forms or abstracted floral motifs, such as the hollyhock or the poppy. "A lamp of Teco ware," wrote a writer in a 1904 issue of *The Craftsman,* "in itself sets off a room, gives that fine, dainty delicate hint of color that is so pleasing to the eye, and soothing to the nerves."

• *1. Conventionalized patterns of floral motif found on a linen textile.* • *2. Placed next to a Grueby vase is a watercolor painting by New York artist Robert Walsh.* • *3. A silver platter is both functional and decorative in this Craftsman home.* • *4. A van Briggle plaque with a metallic finish.*

Furnished with furniture made by Gustav Stickley, Charles Limbert, and the Onodaga Shops, the living room of the Marston House is a showcase of Arts and Crafts movement work.

TOUCHSTONES

The sooner that we appreciated the inevitable, strong, subtle influences, which pass from the eye to the brain, the sooner shall we give to ourselves (and with greater profit to our children than to ourselves) surroundings conducive to plain living and high thinking: rooms in which each object shall have some vital reason for its existence, place and function, and which can form an unobtrusive background for the drama of life.

—*The Craftsman*, 1902

CRAFTSMANSHIP

Craft and craftsmanship is implicit in everything that the Arts and Crafts movement stood for at its genesis and still stands for now. Though we relate to the movement today mostly through the objects that were produced by those who allied themselves with the Arts and Crafts movement, to treat those objects as isolated works of art is to defeat the entire purpose of the movement. In England in the 1880s, the movement began as a rebellion against those who had elevated art to a realm apart from the original meaning of the word "art," that is, of a high level of achieved skill in a craft. The rebellion that led specifically to the Arts and Crafts Exhibition Society began with craftspeople wanting to exhibit their work and not being allowed to do so by members of The Royal Academy who favored the "fine" arts and who preferred to keep to the idea that to follow a craft was to pursue an inferior occupation. The aim of the Arts and Crafts movement was to change the public consciousness regarding art, craft, and craftsmanship, and to revive an appreciation of both the complete process of the making of an object and the level of skill necessary in the creating of that object. In other words, the goal was to engender the awareness that the art in an object should come from the visible skill in its crafting, not from some isolated, refined aesthetic sense of design.

Especially in America, the visibility of craftsmanship became at times more important than the actual craftsmanship. The oddity of it all was that in times before the refining qualities of machines, fine craftsmanship meant removing all visible evidences of handwork; but once the machine could produce a perfectly finished form, retaining a visible memory of the craftsman's work—the hand hammering in the copper of a jardinière, the visible mortise-and-tenon construction of a Limbert chair, the handwoven unevenness of a Craftsman table runner—was once again desirable. This even became odder in the realization that much of what was produced in America around the turn of the century was factory produced.

The ironwork rejas, *the personal brand of Charles Lummis on the El Alisal front door, was designed by the western artist Maynard Dixon. These double doors are nearly seven feet tall, each of them weighing a thousand pounds.*

NATURE

There was a new awareness of nature in the years that followed the Civil War—an awareness of nature as something to be lived in, not conquered. Beginning with Yellowstone in 1872 and followed by Yosemite, Grand Canyon, and Glacier, the national park system began encouraging a new direction of tourism—the great outdoors. Then as city life became more and more congested, the natural world outside assumed the image of an Eden-like retreat from the evils of the modern age, and the countryside, the forest, and the mountains became interconnected with images of family life and home. The idea of nature and images of the natural world became something to be brought into one's home. Wallpaper could express the garden, the roughness of redwood board and batten would evoke a woodland, cobblestones or granite in the fireplace would hold memory of a nearby arroyo or the distant mountains. The grain of the wood in furniture brought to mind the tree from which it was made, and a stencil on a curtain could allude to blossoms in the fields. Reference to nature and the natural world in the home was a rallying against all that was not natural in the modern world—against the machines and people treated as machines, against the isolation that had occurred in daily life from the outdoors, and against the loss of an idealized past lived in a bucolic wonderland.

THE MEDIEVAL

Largely because of the influence of John Ruskin and his work, *The Seven Lamps of Architecture* and *The Stones of Venice* (and within, his oft-quoted chapter "The Nature of Gothic"), the medieval ideal came to be a cornerstone for the Arts and Crafts movement. William Morris, highly influenced by both Ruskin and his writings, saw

Henry Chapman Mercer began building his dream house, Fonthill, in 1908 and worked with eight and sometimes ten laborers over the following four years, using rough sketches rather than architectural drawings and blueprints, forming a structure based on a romanticized vision of a medieval castle.

himself more a thirteenth- than a nine-teenth-century man and modeled his workshops after the early crafts guilds. In America, Charles Rohlfs adopted Gothic references in his carving for his more ornate work, describing it as "imbued with the spirit of the artists in wood of the middle ages." The appeal of the idealized medieval world came from its contrast with the industrial world, which confronted Rohlfs, Morris, Ruskin, and others of the Arts and Crafts movement. This was especially true in the comparison they saw between their idealized vision of the medieval craftsman—trained in a complete skill, able to complete every aspect of a work—and the modern factory worker who is a specialist in only one small aspect of a job

Built from 1910 to 1912, the cloisterlike architecture of the Moravian Pottery and Tile Works was inspired by the Spanish missions of California. Henry Chapman Mercer produced his medieval-inspired tiles here until his death in 1930, after which the tile works continued production into the 1950s. Today the tile works are in operation again, being run as a working museum of Bucks County Department of Parks and Recreation, Pennsylvania.

and who had become, as Morris wrote, "the slave to a machine" and therefore unable to have an appreciation of the total endeavor. The joy in labor had thereby been lost and could only be retrieved by a return to this medieval ideal, to a time of, in Morris's words, "all workmen being artists."

The doors in El Alisal are two-to-four-inches thick, each one unique and handmade from rough-hewn lumber.

Charles Fletcher Lummis (1859–1928).

A Navajo rug found in Lummis's El Alisal.

NATIVE AMERICAN

The Native American culture and artifacts fascinated non-Native Americans as a source of inspiration for craftsmanship and as an idealized image of preindustrial handicrafts. The reality of the Indian nation, though, was far different. By the turn of the century, Native Americans were being forced to conform to the lifestyle of white men who had conquered them and, especially after the Dawes Act of 1887, were steadily losing their tribal lands to the white settlers. Their culture was quickly vanishing and becoming a thing of the past just as they were being romanticized and sentimentalized. Articles on the handicraft of Native Americans were run in *The Craftsman* as well as other magazines of the movement, making suggestions, as in this 1905 article in *The Craftsman,* that "Indian rugs or Navajo blankets lend a touch of comfort and cheer, and the simple designs and primitive colors harmonize as well with trees and vines and the open sky as they do with their native wigwams."

Many individuals studied the Native Americans, collected their artifacts, and advocated use of the objects in their homes. George Wharton James, a Californian and a leader of the Arroyo Guild in Pasadena, researched all

Lummis wrote that he hoped his house would last a thousand years. In a 1907 issue of House Beautiful, *he explained that "First he chose the quaint four-forked sycamore as center of the sixty-by-eighty-foot patio, and in a sense, the shrine of the home. Then he turned mason and set the massive stones in walls from fourteen-to-eighteen-inches thick, mixing the mortar at his individual sand pile. Changing to master craftsman in wood, he burned great logs not less than 400 pounds apiece for raftered ceilings, polishing them down to a soft satin finish."*

aspects of the vanishing Native American cultures and published numerous important books, such as *Indian Basketry and How to Make Baskets* and *What the White Race May Learn From the Indian,* on his findings. Another Californian, Charles Fletcher Lummis, built his Los Angeles home, El Alisal, not only under the influence of his fascination with the Native American cultures but with the actual help of Native American workers. He amassed an important collection of Native American artifacts, founding the Southwest Museum in Los Angeles not only to hold his collection but to carry on with his studies into the Native American cultures.

JAPONISME

After three centuries of self-enforced isolation, Japan was opened to the outside world in 1854 by the arrival of the American flotilla under the command of Commodore Matthew Perry. Having remained sequestered from the advances in industry and technology in the rest of the world, what Commodore Perry found when he sailed into Uraga Bay was a

In Pasadena's historic Bungalow Heaven, a turn-of-the-century bungalow shows the influence of Japan upon exterior architectural details.

country dependent solely upon human and animal power. The industrial abilities that came with the advent of steam, oil, and electrical forms of power had not yet intruded upon what was essentially a medieval society; work was still organized in a noncapitalistic hierarchy within which the craftsman was a more respected member of society than the merchant. The craft being produced by these respected members of society, highly evolved through three hundred years of isolation, had found an inner beauty based on the concepts of simplicity and nature.

When the artifacts of the Japanese were introduced to America in 1876 at the Centennial Exposition in Philadelphia, Victorian Americans were surprised at the quality of workmanship and inherent beauty being produced by this "savage" nation. The high caliber of craftsmanship in the goods the Japanese brought to the exposition stood out in stark contrast to the shoddiness of the American mass-produced goods—the craft items seemed to be a visual statement of John Ruskin's evangelizing about the quality and beauty to be found in preindustrial crafts. There was, in addition, an attraction of the exotic in these Japanese goods—a sensitivity found towards subtle colors and clean lines with asymmetrical placement and an ability to take the forms of nature and conventionalize them into uses for decorative motifs that attracted America. This mastery of the Japanese in creating a simple beauty influenced not only the leading artists and architects of the day but also the average consumer through the household magazines and design periodicals.

A number of Arts and Crafts architects and designers collected not just Japanese goods but the handmade wood-block prints that so differed from the western artistic sensibility. Frank Lloyd Wright, Harvey Ellis, and Charles Sumner Greene all collected these prints, using them not just as wall decorations but as educational sources of design.

From this meeting of East and West came several unique styles of homes and interiors. Frank Lloyd Wright took the clean, simple geometric principles from the Japanese print and utilized it to form the foundation of much that was valued in the Modernist movement. His buildings were not Japanese but had an essence of Japan in them that came from his mastery of the spatial senses of the Japanese room. He organized his interiors with an openness reminiscent of the Japanese interiors, which could take small rooms and expansively open them up by means of sliding *fusuma* doors. To Wright, materials did not matter; thus, he was free to employ this learned language of architecture with the use of concrete and steel, forming a truly new design sense.

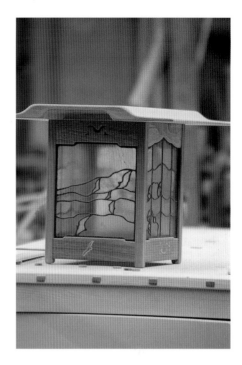

A modern-day construction of one of the original designs of Greene and Greene, by James Ipekjian of James Randell Company.

Accessories & Miscellaneous

Andrus, Mitchell
68 Central Avenue
Stirling, NJ 07980
(908) 647-7442
www.mitchellandrus.com

Ark Antiques
(antique jewelry)
PO Box 3133
New Haven, CT 06515
(203) 498-8572

The Arts and Crafts Press
(letterpress printed note cards)
8019 SE Culver Street
Olalla, WA 98359
(360) 871 7707
www.artsandcraftspress.com

Arts and Crafts Tours
110 Riverside Drive, Suite 15E
New York, NY 10024
(212) 362-0761
artscraftstours@aol.com

Carol Mead Design (stationery)
www.carolmead.com

Cranberry Press
HC66, PO Box 119A Main Street
Kingston, NM 88042
(877) 653-7746
www.cranberrypress.com

Crestwood Designs
512 Crestwood Court
Highlands, Victoria, BC
V9B 6J3
(250) 474-5332
www.CrestwoodDesign.com

Dalton's American Decorative Arts
(china)
1931 James Street
Syracuse, NY 13206
(315) 463-1568
www.daltons.com

Dard Hunter Studios
PO Box 771
Chillicothe, OH 45601
(740) 774-1236
www.dardhunter.com

El Dorado
3603 Polk Street
Houston, TX 77003
(713) 529-3880
www.eldoradowoodworks.com

Fair Oak Workshops
PO Box 5578
River Forest, IL 60305
(800) 341-0597
www.fairoak.com

Fine Lines (frames)
PO Box 412
Belvidere, NJ 07823
(800) 294-7973
www.finelinesframing.com

FMG Design
2601 West Farwell Avenue
Chicago, IL 60645
(773) 761-2957
www.fmgdesigns.com

Holton Frames
5515 Doyle Street, #2
Emeryville, CA 94608
(800) 250-5277
(510) 450-0350
holtonframes.com

Jerry Cook Antiques
2515 North Bethel
Olympia, WA 98506
(360) 754-8362

The Legacy Bookshop & Gallery
654 Main Street
East Aurora, NY 14052
(716) 652-6797

Mettle Works (Arts and Crafts jewelry)
Route 1, PO Box 243
Carmel, CA 93923
(831) 624-8027

Old Ways Limited
39 Barton Avenue SE
Minneapolis, MN 55414
(612) 379-2142
www.oldwaysltd.com

Oregon Copper Bowl Company
PO Box 5859
Eugene, OR 97405
(541) 485-9845
www.oregoncopperbowl.com

P22 Type Foundry
PO Box 770
Buffalo, NY 14213
(800) 722-5080
www.p22.com

Present Time Clocks
18452 Skagit City Road
Mt. Vernon, WA 98273
(360) 445-4702
www.present-time-clocks.com

Rustic Spirit
(866) 649-4799
www.rusticspirit.com

United Crafts
127 West Putnam Avenue,
Suite 123
Greenwich, CT 06830
(203) 869-4898
www.unitedcrafts.com

White Rabbit Wood Works
30370 - 438 Avenue
Yankton, SD 57078
(605) 665-3800
www.whiterabbet.com

White, Sarah
127 West Putnam Avenue,
Suite 123
Greenwich, CT 06830
(203) 869-4898
www.unitedcrafts.com

Architects, Architectural Consultants & Interior Designers

Andersen, Tim, Architect
7726 33rd Avenue NE
Seattle, WA 98115
(206) 524-8841
timsen@comcast.net

Architectural Detail
299 North Altadena Drive
Pasadena, CA 91107
(626) 844-6670

Ashmore/Kessenich Design
6336 NE Garfield Street
Portland, OR 97211
(503) 286-6258
www.bungalowpros.com

The Building Biographer
400 East California Boulevard, #3
Pasadena, CA 91106
(626) 792-7465
timgregory@sbcglobal.net

Duchscherer, Paul
303A Roosevelt Way
San Francisco, CA 94114
(415) 861-6256
www.artisticlicense.org

Gandsey, Mary
(repair, refinishing, painting)
(626) 797-3090

Griffin, Robert
One Village Lane
Asheville, NC 28803
(828) 274-5979

Heinz, Thomas A.
3217 Central Street
Evanston, IL 60201
(847) 328-6552
taharch@earthlink.net

Interior Vision
(Consulting anywhere!)
PO Box 867
Port Townsend, WA 98368
(888) 385-3161
(360) 385-3161
www.interiorvision.com
karenintvision@aol.com

Ivy Hill Interiors
3920 SW 109th Street
Seattle, WA 98146
(206) 243-6768

John Benriter Preservation & Restoration
2300 Stonyvale Road
Angeles National Forest
Tujunga, CA 91042
(818) 353-1136

The Johnson Partnership
1212 NE 65th Street
Seattle, WA 98115
(206) 523-1618
www.tjp.us

Kessenich-Tesmer Design
617 Grant Street
Fort Atkinson, WI 53538
(920) 563-6570
(608) 213-4627
www.bungalowpros.com

Makinson, Randell
233 North Grand Avenue
Pasadena, CA 91103
(626) 449-4600
makinson@earthlink.net

Marrin, James
99 South Raymond Avenue,
Suite 401
Pasadena, CA 91105
(626) 577-4084
designmarrin@earthlink.net

Matthew Bialecki Associates
108 Main Street
New Paltz, NY 12561
(845) 255-6276
www.mbialeckiarch.com

Miller, Clinton M., & Associates
920 Federal Avenue East
Seattle, WA 98102
(206) 329-8511
cmmiller1@qwest.net

Morosco, Gerald Lee, AIA
1819 East Carson Street
Pittsburgh, PA 15203
(412) 431-4347
www.glm-architects.com

Polsky, Jared, & Associates
469B Magnolia Avenue
Larkspur, CA 94939
(415) 927-1156

Rissetto, Peter Lee
18 Plum Brook Road
Katonah, NY 10536
(914) 232-7911
prissetto99@aol.com

SALA Architects
43 Main Street SE, Suite 410
Minneapolis, MN 55414
(612) 379-3037
www.salaarc.com

S. M. Stemper Architects
217 Pine Street, #700
Seattle, WA 98101
(206) 624-2777

Terpstra Design Associates
5510 Cascade Road, #260
Grand Rapids, MI 49546
(616) 949-6300
www.pola-arch.com

Wai/Gorny
1029 NE 62nd Street
Seattle, WA 98115
(206) 523-8125
www.waigorny.com

Artists and Artwork

The Arts and Crafts Press
(block prints)
8019 SE Culver Street
Olalla, WA 98359
(360) 871-7707
www.artsandcraftspress.com

Bojanowski, Tom
45 South Grove Street
East Aurora, NY 14052
(716) 652-9353
tomboj@buffnet.net

Dry Creek Art Press
1321 South Broadway
Denver, CO 80210
(303) 956-2994
www.dcartpress.com

Ehrens, Susan
(turn-of-the-century photographs)
PO Box 11143
Oakland, CA 94611
(510) 658-9087

Killion, Tom (wood-block prints)
PO Box 1028
Pt. Reyes Station, CA 94956
(415) 663-1516
www.tomkillion.com

Laura Wilder Artwork
103 Richland Street
Rochester, NY 14609
(585) 288-1089
www.laurawilder.com

Nejko, Paulette
PO Box 735
Camden, ME 04843
(207) 230-0390
www.gnidziejkogallery.com/paulette

Steven Thomas Inc.
PO Box 41
Woodstock, VT 05091
(802) 457-1764
www.woodblock-prints.com

Stewart, Brian (plein-air painting)
5321 Xerxes South
Minneapolis, MN 55410
(612) 920-4653
www.stew-art.com

West, Kathleen
PO Box 545
159 Maple Street
East Aurora, NY 14052
(716) 652-9125
www.kathleenwest.com

William McCarthy Fine Art
139 Gillies Road
Hamden, CT 06517
(203) 230-8235
www.williammccarthyfineart.com

Auctions

Bonhams & Butterfields
Main Gallery
7601 Sunset Boulevard
Los Angeles, CA 90046
(323) 850-7500
www.butterfields.com

Christie's
20 Rockefeller Plaza
New York, NY 10022
(212) 636-2000
www.christies.com

David Rago Craftsman Auctions
333 North Main Street
Lambertville, NJ 08530
(609) 397-9374
www.ragoarts.com

Fontaine's Auction Gallery
1485 West Housatonic
Pittsfield, MA 01201
(413) 488-8922
www.fontaineauction.com

John Toomey Gallery
818 North Boulevard
Oak Park, IL 60301
(708) 383-5234
www.treadwaygallery.com

Skinner, Inc.
The Heritage on the Garden
63 Park Plaza
Boston, MA 02116
(617) 350-5400
www.skinnerinc.com

Sotheby's
1334 York Avenue
New York, NY 10021
(541) 312-5682
www.sothebys.com

Swann Galleries, Inc.
104 East 25th Street
New York, NY 10010
(212) 254-4710
www.swanngalleries.com

Arts & Crafts Antique Dealers

1904 Antiques & Design
8027 SE 13th Avenue
Portland, OR 97202
(503) 235-9944
arts-antiques@comcast.net

A. Gallarano Gallery
81B North Washington Street
Berkeley Springs, WV 25411
(304) 258-0815
www.agallaranogallery.com

A Mission Oak Shop
1645 Tenth Avenue East, #302
Seattle, WA 98102
(206) 941-6813
(206) 323-5246
www.missionoakshop.com

Antique Articles
PO Box 72
North Billerica, MA 01862
(978) 649-4983
www.antiquearticles.com

Antique Quest
513 Broadway Ave
Toronto, ON M4G 2R7
(416) 429-5591

Ark Antiques (antique jewelry)
PO Box 3133
New Haven, CT 06515
(203) 498-8572
ark_antiques@yahoo.com

Art Moderne Antiques
1503 East Henry Avenue
Tampa, FL 33610
(813) 237-8092

Austin Craftsman
1015 Palomino
San Marcos, TX 78666
(512) 415-3005
www.austincraftsman.com

Bennett, Joyce and Rich
PO Box 351, C.V.H. #16
Middletown, CT 06457
(860) 343-9514

Berman Gallery
441 South Jackson Street Media
Philadelphia, PA 19063
(888) 784-2554
(215) 733-0707
www.bermangallery.com

Bettinger, Robert
PO Box 333
Mt. Dora, FL 32756
(352) 735-3575
www.robertbettinger.com

Carol Eppel Antiques
124 2nd Street South
Stillwater, MN 55082
(651) 351-2888
caeppel@aol.com

Cathers & Dembrosky
43 East 10th Street
New York, NY 10003
(212) 353-1244
www.cathers-dembrosky.com

Cavanaugh, Tom
8155 Gulf Boulevard
Navarre Beach, FL 32566
(850) 936-1097

Cavanaugh, Tom (summer address)
The Bay Street Studio
6 Bay Street
Boothbay Harbor, ME 04538
(207) 633-3186

Cherry Tree Antiques
1045 Parkridge Road
Hillsboro, MO 63050
(888) 313-1765
(314) 797-5144
oberarts@ix.netcom.com

Chestnut Street Antiques
44 Sebastopol Road
Santa Rosa, CA 95407
(707) 579-8488

Circa 1910 Antiques
7206 Melrose Avenue
Los Angeles, CA 90046
(323) 965-1910
www.circa1910antiques.com

Circa 87
69 Jefferson Street
Stamford, CT 06902
(203) 968-6485

Craftsman Antiques
Phil Chun
5701 Telegraph Avenue
Oakland, CA 94609
(510) 595-7977
crftman@pacbell.net

The Craftsman Home
Lee Jester
3048 Claremont Avenue
Berkeley, CA 94705
(510) 655-6503
www.craftsmanhome.com

Crones Collectibles
PO Box 2306
Brewster, MA 02631
(508) 896-5038
www.cronescollectibles.com

Dalton's American Decorative Arts
1931 James Street
Syracuse, NY 13206
(315) 463-1568
www.daltons.com

Detelich Arts and Crafts Gallery
1654 Ocean Avenue
Santa Monica, CA 90401
(800) 595-8192
(310) 260-9667
www.detelichgallery.com

Drucker Antiques
487 East Main Street, Suite 197
Mt. Kisco, NY 10549
(914) 923-4560
www.druckerantiques.com

E-Modern
Chris Kennedy
PO Box 751
North Hampton, MA 01061
(800) 336-3376
www.e-modern.net

Edwards Antiques
PO Box 364
89 Hillsboro Street
Pittsboro, NC 27312
(919) 542-5649
antiques@centernet.net

The Emporium
1800 Westheimer
Houston, TX 77098
(713) 528-3808
www.the-emporium.com

Farmers and Merchants Gallery
PO Box 615, On the Square
Pilot Point, TX 76258
(940) 686-2396

Eric Firestone Gallery
4425 North Campbell Avenue
Tucson, AZ 85718
(520) 577-7711
www.ericfirestonegallery.com

Gallery 532
142 Duane Street
New York, NY 10013
(877) 425-5532
(212) 964-1282
www.gallery532.com

Geoffrey Diner Gallery
1730 21st Street NW
Washington, DC 20009
(202) 483-5005
www.dinergallery.com

The Handwerk Shop
PO Box 22455
Portland, OR 97222
(503) 659-0914
www.thehandwerkshop.com

Heartwood
956 Cherry Street
Grand Rapids, MI 49506
(616) 454-1478

Hill House Antiques
276 South Undermountain Road
Sheffield, MA 01257
(413) 229-2374
www.hillhouseantiques.com

The House 1860–1925
6–10 St. James Street
Monmouth, U.K. NP25 3DL
01600-772721
www.thehouse1860-1925.com/

House of Orange
Alameda, CA
(510) 523-3378

Hunt, Nancy
PO Box 81
Manakin-Sabot, VA 23103
(804) 784-3155
stschnzer@aol.com

Isak Lindenauer Antiques
4143 19th Street
San Francisco, CA 94114
(415) 552-6436

Jerry Cook Antiques
(360) 754-8362

JMW Gallery
144 Lincoln Street
Boston, MA 02111
(617) 338-9097
www.jmwgallery.com

Jack Moore American Arts &
Crafts Antiques
1419 North Lake Avenue
Pasadena, CA 91104

Jack Pap Antiques
PO Box 322
West Simsbury, CT 06092
(860) 658-4374

Jean Bragg Antiques
3901 Magazine Street
New Orleans, LA 70115
(504) 895-7375
www.jeanbraggantiques.com

John Toomey Gallery
818 North Boulevard
Oak Park, IL 60301
(708) 383-5234
www.treadwaygallery.com

Leah Gordon Manhattan Art &
Antiques Center
1050 Second Ave, Gallery 18
New York, NY 10022
(212) 872-1422
www.leahgordon.com

Lifetime Gallery
7506 Santa Monica Boulevard
Los Angeles, CA 90046
(323) 876-8464

Linda Davidson Antiques
726 East Lakeshore Drive
Landrum, SC 29356
(864) 457-5239
webpages.charter.net/davidsons

McIlwain, Craig
2711 Albon Road
Maumee, OH 43537
(419) 861-3601

Mark Heckhoff Antiques
550 Upper Mountain Road
New Hope, PA 18938
(215) 794-9490
heckoff@hotmail.com

McCormack & Company
245 Birdkey Drive
Sarasota, FL 34236
(941) 350-2785

Michael FitzSimmons
Decorative Arts
311 West Superior Street
Chicago, IL 60610
(312) 787-0496
www.fitzdecarts.com

Mission Oak Shop
109 Main Street
Putnam, CT 06260
(860) 928-6662
www.artsncrafts.com

North Park Craftsman/Tap
Lighting
3690 6th Avenue
San Diego, CA 92103
(619) 295-5958
www.northparkcraftsman.com

Ouroboros Art Pottery
10203 Chamberlain Road
Mechanicsville, VA 23116
(804) 730-8004

Partition Street Antiques
114 Partition Street
Saugerties, NY 12477
(800) 948-8567
(845) 246-1800
www.partitionstreetantiques.com

Pearce Fox Decorative Arts
162 North 3rd Street
Philadelphia, PA 19106
(610) 688-3678
www.foxmission.com

Perrault-Rago Gallery
333 North Main Street
Lambertville, NJ 08530
(609) 397-1802
www.ragoarts.com/prgallery.html

Pete's Pots
PO Box 2724
Norcross, GA 30091
(770) 446-1419
www.petespots.com
www.gustavstickley.com

Peter-Roberts Antiques
39 Bond Street
New York, NY 10012
(212) 477-9690
pra.nyc@verizon.net

Phil Taylor Antiques
224 Fox-Sauk Road
Ottumwa, IA 52501
(641) 682-7492
ptaylorantiques@pcsia.net

The Plastic Arts
(speaker on ceramics)
301 Austin
Jackson, MI 49202
(517) 782-9910

Raymond Groll Metalman
PO Box 421, Station A
Flushing, NY 11358
(718) 463-0059
www.stores.ebay.com/raymondgroll

Roland, Leah
Split Personality
PO Box 419
Leonia, NJ 07605
(201) 947-1535
(201) 947-2291
splitpersonality@verizon.net

Silverman's Selected Antiques
1323 Oak Fanfare
San Antonio, TX 78258
(210) 481-9486
nmsilver@aol.com

Smith, Colin C.
5309 Jackson Street
Omaha, NE 68106
(402) 551-5018
(by appointment only)

So Rare! Galleries
Triangle Building, Suite 504
701 Smithfield Street
Pittsburgh, PA 15222
(800) 260-2909
(412) 281-5150
www.so-rare.com

South Pointe Antiques
Route 272 & Denver Road
Adamstown, PA 19501
(717) 484-1026

Spotted Horse Collectibles
Tina and Mark Richey
12141 Couch Mill Road
Knoxville, TN 37932
(865) 690-7221
shcollect@aol.com

Stuart F. Solomon Antiques
9 3/4 Market Street
Northampton, MA 01060
(800) 883-5400
(413) 586-7776
www.ssolomon.com

Surgan, David
(specialist in Heintz cut metal)
328 Flatbush Avenue, PMB 123
Brooklyn, NY 11238
(718) 638-3768
surgheintz@aol.com

Terry Seger Arts and Crafts
880 Foxcreek Lane
Cincinnati, OH 45233
(513) 941-9689
jtseger@fuse.net

Textile Artifacts
Paul Freeman and Nancy Eaton
12575 Crenshaw Boulevard
Hawthorne, CA 90250
(310) 676-2424
www.archiveedition.com

Thomas, Steven
PO Box 41
Woodstock, VT 05091
(802) 457-1764
www.woodblock-prints.com

Threshold Antiques
Mass Antiques Coop, MA
(617) 244-8605

Tim Gleason Gallery
194 Elizabeth Street, #2
New York, NY 10012
(212) 966-5777
www.timgleasongallery.com

Treadway Gallery Inc.
2029 Madison Road
Cincinnati, OH 45208
(513) 321-6742
www.treadwaygallery.com

Verlangieri Gallery
PO Box 844
Cambria, CA 93428
(805) 927-4428

Voorhees Craftsman
1415 North Lake Avenue
Pasadena, CA 91104
(888) 982-6377
www.voorheescraftsman.com

White, Doug and Paula
2042 North Rio Grande Avenue, #E
Orlando, FL 32804
(407) 839-0004
www.A-1auction.net

Carpets & Rugs

Blue Hills
400 Woodland Way
Greenville, SC 29607
(864) 232-4217

Claremont Rug Company
6087 Claremont Avenue
Oakland, CA 94618
(510) 654-0816
www.claremontrugs.com

The Craftsman Home
3048 Claremont Avenue
Berkeley, CA 94705
(510) 655-6503
www.craftsmanhome.com

Fair Oak Workshops
PO Box 5578
River Forest, IL 60305
(800) 341-0597
www.fairoak.com

J. R. Burrows & Company
PO Box 522
Rockland, MA 02370
(800) 347-1795
www.burrows.com

Jax Rugs
109 Parkway
Berea, KY 40403
(859) 986-5410
www.jaxrugs.com

Michaelian and Kohlberg, Inc.
578 Broadway, 2nd floor
New York, NY 10012
(212) 431-9009
www.michaelian.com

New River Artisans, Inc.
528 Piney Creek School Road
Piney Creek, NC 28663
(336) 359-2216
www.newriverartisans.com

The Persian Carpet, Inc.
5634 Chapel Hill Boulevard
Durham, NC 27707
(800) 333-1801
www.artsandcraftscarpets.com

Furniture

A. K. A. Drake Custom Furniture
David B. "Drake" Adkisson
619 Western Avenue, #117
Seattle, WA 98104
(206) 467-1761

Andrus, Mitchell
68 Central Avenue
Stirling, NJ 07980
(908) 647-7442
www.mitchellandrus.com

AppleTree WoodWorks
604 East Cossitt Avenue
La Grange, IL 60525
(708) 579-0369
www.appletree-woodworks.com

Berkeley Mills
2830 Seventh Street
Berkeley, CA 94710
(510) 549-2854
www.berkeleymills.com

Black River Mission
Paul and Bonita Varney
PO Box 146
Milford, NY 13807
(607) 286-7641
www.blackrivermission.com

Brotherton, Todd
PO Box 404
Mt. Shasta, CA 96067
(530) 938-4000
toddb@snowcrest.net

Bertucci, Dennis
PO Box 1520
Boulder, UT 84716
(435) 335-7392

Byer Woodworking & Company
136 East St. Joseph Street, Unit E
Arcadia, CA 91006
(626) 445-7451
www.byerwoodworking.com

Caledonia Studios
1601 18th Street
Oakland, CA 94607
(510) 839-5569
www.caledoniastudios.com

Catskill Custom Carpentry
Robert Allen
11 Field Court
Kingston, NY 12401
(845) 339-8029
www.catskillfurniture.com

Cherry Valley Furniture
887 Rutledge Avenue
Charleston, SC 29403
(800) 763-2050
www.cherryvalleyfurniture.com

The Craftsman Home
3048 Claremont Avenue
Berkeley, CA 94705
(510) 655-6503
www.craftsmanhome.com

Crestwood Designs
240 Old Mossy Road
Highlands, Victoria, BC V9B 6J3
(250) 474-5332
www.crestwooddesign.com

David B. Hellman Associates
PO Box 526
Watertown, MA 02471
(617) 923-4829
www.dbhellman.com

El Dorado Woodworks
3603 Polk Street
Houston, TX 77003
(713) 529-3880
www.eldoradowoodworks.com

Floating Stone Wood Works
88 Hatch Street, Loft 406
New Bedford, MA 02745
(800) 267-1079
www.floatingstonewoodworks.com

James Ipekjian Custom Woodwork
768 North Fair Oaks Avenue
Pasadena, CA 91103
(626) 792-5025

Kevin Rodel Furniture
& Design Studio
44 Leighton Road
Pownal, ME 04069
(207) 688-4483

Krueger, Brian
c/o Graham Lee Associates
2870 East 54th Street
Vernon, CA 90058
(323) 581-8203 ext. 11
www.grahamlee.com

Laberge, William
5145 Route 30
Dorset, VT 05251
(802) 325-2117
www.williamlaberge.com

Mission Evolution
Arnold d'Empagnier
(301) 384-3201
www.missionevolution.com

Old Ways Limited
39 Barton Avenue SE
Minneapolis, MN 55414
(612) 379-2142
www.oldwaysltd.com

Paul Downs Cabinet Makers
401 East 4th Street
Bldg. 8, 4th floor
Bridgeport, PA 19405
(610) 664-9902
www.pauldowns.com

Peart, Darrell
3419 C Street NE, #16
Auburn, WA 98002
(425) 277-4070
www.furnituremaker.com

Raven Vale Gallery, LLC
657 Trumbull Avenue SE
Warren, OH 44484
(330) 369-4491
www.ravenvale.com

Raymond Tillman
9 Fairview Avenue
Chatham, NY 12037
(518) 392-4603

RB WoodWorking
Rick Badgley
43812 Sierra Drive
Three Rivers, CA 93271
(559) 561-4823
www.rbwoodworking.com

Robert Lock Studio
15802 West Marie Avenue
Prairie View, IL 60069
(847) 808-0856
www.robertlockstudio.com

Shortridge Company, Ltd.
(Craftsman children furniture)
504 South Charlotte Avenue
Sioux Falls, SD 57103
(888) 335-3393
www.shortridgeltd.com

Stangeland, Thomas
309 8th Avenue North
Seattle, WA 98109
(206) 622-2004
www.artistcraftsman.net

The Stickley Company
PO Box 480
Manlius, NY 13104
(315) 682-5500
www.stickley.com

Swartzendruber Hardwood
Creations
1100 Chicago Avenue
Goshen, IN 46528
(800) 531-2502
www.swartzendruber.com

Strictly Mission
3946 Lanark Road
Coopersburg, PA 18036
(610) 814-3065
www.strictlymission.com

Thomas Moser Cabinetmakers
PO Box 1237
Auburn, ME 04211
(800) 708-9703
www.thosmoser.com

Tim Celeski Studios
6743 Beach Drive SW
Seattle, WA 98136
(206) 932-4466
www.celeski.com

Trustworth Studios
PO Box 1109
Plymouth, MA 02362
(508) 746-1847
www.trustworth.com

Voorhees Craftsman
1415 North Lake Avenue
Pasadena, CA 91104
(888) 982-6377
www.voorheescraftsman.com

Glass & Stained Glass

Anne Ryan Miller Glass Studio
PO Box 566
Nashville, IN 47448
(812) 988-9766
www.anneryanmillerglassstudio.com

Architectural Artworks
Susan McCracken
PO Box 8821
Atlanta, GA 31106
(404) 223-3280
www.architecturalartworks.net

Brian McNally Glass Artist
3236 Calle Piñon
Santa Barbara, CA 93105
(805) 687-7212
brianmcnallyglassartist@cox.net

Hamm Glass Studio
6737 Bright Avenue
Whittier, CA 90602
(562) 696-2883
www.hammstudios.com

The Judson Stained Glass Studio
200 South Avenue 66
Los Angeles, CA 90042
(800) 445-8376
(323) 255-0131
www.judsonstudios.com

Lundberg Studios
PO Box C
Davenport, CA 95017
(888) 423-9711
(831) 423-2532
www.lundbergstudios.com

Theodore Ellison Designs
1248 International Boulevard
Oakland, CA 94606
(510) 534-7632
www.theodoreellison.com

Tippers Willow Glass Studio
George Zajicek
PO Box 680
Nashville, IN 47448
(812) 988-7096
www.tipperswillow.com

Hardware

Architectural Detail
2449 White Street
Pasadena, CA 91107
(626) 844-6670

Arts and Crafts Hardware
28011 Malvina
Warren, MI 48088
(586) 772-7279
www.arts-n-craftshardware.com

Ball and Ball Hardware
463 West Lincoln Highway
Exton, PA 19341
(800) 257-3711

Classic Accents
PO Box 1181
Southgate, MI 48195
(800) 245-7742
www.classicaccents.net

Craftsman Hardware
(360) 403-7202
www.craftsmanhardware.com

Crown City Hardware
1047 North Allen Avenue
Pasadena, CA 91104
(800) 950-1047
(626) 794-1188
www.crowncityhardware.com

Eugenia's Place Antique Hardware
5370 Peachtree Road
Chamblee, GA 30341
(770) 458-1677
www.eugeniaantiquehardware.com

Horton Brasses Inc.
49 Nooks Hill Road
Cromwell, CT 06416
(800) 754-9127
(860) 635-4400
www.horton-brasses.com

International Door & Latch
191 Seneca Road
Eugene, OR 97402
(541) 686-5647
www.internationaldoor.com

Liz's Antique Hardware
453 South La Brea
Los Angeles, CA 90036
(323) 939-4403
www.lahardware.com

Oak Park Home and Hardware
133 North Oak Park Avenue
Oak Park, IL 60301
(708) 445-3606
www.oakparkhome-hardware.com

Renovator's Supply
(800) 659-2211
www.rensup.com

Vintage Hardware
181 Lost Lake Lane
Campbell, CA 95009
(408) 246-9918
www.vintagehardware.com

Lighting

Andrus, Mitchell
68 Central Avenue
Stirling, NJ 07980
(908) 647-7442
www.mitchellandrus.com

Archive Designs
3762 West 11th Avenue, #264
Eugene, OR 97402
(541) 607-6581
www.archivedesigns.com

Arroyo Craftsman
4509 Little John Street
Baldwin Park, CA 91706
(626) 960-9411
www.arroyo-craftsman.com

Aurora Studios
Michael Adams
3064 County Route 176
Oswego, NY 13126
(315) 343-0339
www.aurorastudios.com

Berry, Karl
265 Douglas Street
Brooklyn, NY 11217
(718) 596-1419

Brass Light Gallery
PO Box 674
Milwaukee, WI 53201
(800) 243-9595
www.brasslight.com

Conant Custom Brass
270 Pine Street
Burlington, VT 05401
(802) 658-4482
www.conantcustombrass.com

Copperwood Lantern
12715 Thunder
Mountain Road
Valleyford, WA 99036
(509) 228-9342

The Craftsman Home
3048 Claremont Avenue
Berkeley, CA 94705
(510) 655-6503
www.craftsmanhome.com

Evergreen Studios
6543 Alpine Drive SW
Olympia, WA 98512
(360) 352-0694
www.evergreenstudios.com

Historic Lighting
114 East Lemon Avenue
Monrovia, CA 91016
(888) 757-9770
(626) 303-4899
www.historiclighting.com

James Ipekjian Custom Woodwork
768 North Fair Oaks Avenue
Pasadena, CA 91103
(626) 792-5025

Luminaria
154 South Madison
Spokane, WA 99201
(800) 638-5619
www.luminaria.com

Lundberg Studios
PO Box C
Davenport, CA 95017
(831) 423-2532
www.lundbergstudios.com

Metro Lighting and Crafts
2216 San Pablo Avenue
Berkeley, CA 94702
(510) 540-0509

Mica Lamp Company
517 State Street
Glendale, CA 91203
(800) 90-Lamps

Oak Park Home and
Hardware
133 North Oak Park Avenue
Oak Park, IL 60301
(708) 445-3606
www.oakparkhome-hardware.com

Old California Lantern Company
975 North Enterprise Street
Orange, CA 92867
(800) 577-6679
www.oldcalifornia.com

William Morris Lamps
1716 Ellie Court
Benicia, CA 94510
(707) 745-3907
www.williammorrisstudio.com

Metalwork

Aurora Studios
(860) 928-6662
www.artsncrafts.com

Archive Designs
3762 West 11th Avenue, #264
Eugene, OR 97402
(541) 607-6581
www.archivedesigns.com

Arnold Benetti, Coppersmith
(415) 567-2107
www.arnoldbenettistudio.
homestead.com

The Aurora Silversmith
PO Box 140
East Aurora, NY 14052
(716) 652-6043

Historic Arts and Casting
5580 West Bagley Park Road
West Jordan, UT 84088
(800) 225-1414
www.historicalarts.com

John Welch/Metalwork
4920 Lone Lake Road
Langley, WA 98260
(360) 321-2293

Linkasink
(866) 395-8377
www.linkasink.com

Surgan, David
(specialist in Heintz cut metal)
328 Flatbush Avenue, PMB 123
Brooklyn, NY 11238
(718) 638-3768
surgheintz@aol.com

Tillman, Raymond
9 Fairview Avenue
Chatham, NY 12037
(518) 392-4603

United Crafts
127 West Putnam Avenue,
Suite 123
Greenwich, CT 06830
(203) 869-4898
www.unitedcrafts.com

Pottery & Tiles

Alchemie Ceramics
1550 Grascony Road
Leucadia, CA 92024
(760) 942-6051

American Art Pottery Association
www.amartpot.org

The Arts & Clay Company
280 Tinker Street
Woodstock, NY 12498
(845) 679-6875

American Art Pottery
129 Market Street
Portsmouth, NH 03801
(207) 251-0452

Common Ground Pottery
221 Bram Street
Madison, WI 53713
(608) 255-2744
www.commongroundpottery.com

Craftsman Studios
4425 4th Avenue NE
Seattle, WA 98105
(206) 632-7976
www.craftsman-studios.com

David Ross Ceramics
575 Solano Avenue
Sonoma, CA 95476
(707) 996-2192
www.artisanknobs.com

Dedham Pottery and
Chelsea Pottery
248 Highland Street
Dedham, MA 02026
(800) 283-8070
www.dedhampottery.com

Designs in Tile
PO Box 358
Mount Shasta, CA 96067
(530) 926-2629
www.designsintile.com

Door Pottery
PO Box 14557
Madison, WI 53708
(608) 240-1626
www.doorpottery.com

Doty, Riley
(restoration work and tile setting)
2179 East 27th Street
Oakland, CA 94606
(510) 261-1122

Duquella Tile
PO Box 90065
Portland, OR 97290
(866) 218-8221
(503) 256-8330
www.tiledecorative.com

Ephraim Faience Pottery
PO Box 168
Deerfield, WI 53531
(888) 704-7687
www.ephraimpottery.com

Gordon, Leah
1050 Second Avenue
New York, NY 10022
(212) 872-1422
www.leahgordon.com

Handcraft Tile
1696 South Main Street
Milpitas, CA 95035
(877) 262-1140
(408) 262-1140
www.handcrafttile.com

Hunter Davis Studio
16021 North Chronicle Lane
Colbert, WA 99005
(509) 238-3275
www.hunterdavisstudio.com

Jean Bragg Antiques
3901 Magazine Street
New Orleans, LA 70115
(504) 895-7375
www.jeanbraggantiques.com

Just Art Pottery
6606 North Rustic Oak Court
Peoria, IL 61614
(309) 690-7966
www.justartpottery.com

Laguna 20th Century
American Art Pottery
116 South Washington Street
Pioneer Square
Seattle, WA 98104
(206) 682-6162
www.lagunapottery.com

Maverick Historical
Fountains & Tiles
4 Conchas Place
Santa Fe, NM 87508
(505) 466-1950
www.maverickfountains.com

Mcintyre Tile
PO Box 14
Healdsburg, CA 95448
(707) 433-8866
www.mcintyre-tile.com

The Moravian
Pottery and Tile Work
East Court Street
Doylestown, PA 18901
(215) 348-9461
www.mercermuseum.org

Motawi Tileworks
170 Enterprise Drive
Ann Arbor, MI 48103
(734) 213-0017
www.motawi.com

Ontko, Janet
PO Box 4356
Fresno, CA 93744
(559) 230-1855
www.janetontko.com

Ouroboros Art Pottery
10203 Chamberlain Road
Mechanicsville, VA 23116
(804) 730-8004

Perrault-Rago Gallery
333 North Main Street
Lambertville, NJ 08530
(609) 397-9374
www.ragoarts.com/prgallery.html

Pewabic Pottery (1903–1961,
founded by Mary Chase Perry
Stratton)
10125 East Jefferson
Detriot, MI 48214
(313) 822-0954
www.pewabic@pewabic.com

Pratt and Larson Ceramics
1201 SE 3rd Avenue
Portland, OR 97214
(503) 231-9464

Richard Thomas Keit Studios
(by appointment only)
206 Canada Street
Ojai, CA 93023
(805) 640-9360
www.rtkstudios.com

Rocheford Handmade Tile
3315 Garfield Avenue South
Minneapolis, MN 55408
(612) 824-6216
www.housenumbertiles.com

Roycroft Potters
37 South Grove Street
East Aurora, NY 14052
(716) 652-7422
www.roycroftpotters.com

Solomon, Malvina
1021 Lexington Avenue
New York, NY 10021
(212) 535-5200

Terracroft Tiles
3048 Claremont Avenue
Berkeley, CA 94705
(510) 655-6503
www.craftsmanhome.com

Tile Antiques
PO Box 4505
Seattle, WA 98194
(206) 632-9675
tileantiques@comcast.net

Tile Heritage Foundation
PO Box 1850
Healdsburg, CA 95448
(707) 431-8453
www.tileheritage.org

Publications

The Arts and Crafts Press
(letterpress publishing of books
about the Arts & Crafts
movement)
8019 SE Culver Street
Olalla, WA 98359
(360) 871-7707
www.artsandcraftspress.com

Clinker Press
240 North Grand Avenue
Pasadena, CA 91103
(626) 792-9729
www.typeandstitch.com

Knock On Wood Publications
25 Upper Brush Creek Road
Fletcher, NC 28732
(828) 628-1915
www.arts-craftsconference.com

Old-House Interiors
PO Box 56009
Boulder, CO 80322
(800) 462-0211
www.oldhouseinteriors.com

Old House Journal
(800) 234-3797
www.oldhousejournal.com

Style 1900
333 North Main Street
Lambertville, NJ 08530
(609) 397-4104
www.style1900.com

The Tabby: A Chronicle of The
Arts & Crafts Movement
8019 SE Culver Street
Olalla, WA 98359
(360) 871-7707
www.artsandcraftspress.com

Turn of the Century Editions
The Parchment Press
38 Hickory Drive
Maplewood, NJ 07040
(973) 275-9703
www.turnofthecenturyeditions.com

Stores & Shops

American Furnishing Company
1409 West Third Avenue
Columbus, OH 43212
(614) 488-7263
www.americanfurnishings.com

AppleTree WoodWorks
604 East Cossitt Avenue
La Grange, IL 60525
(708) 579-0369
www.appletree-woodworks.com

The Arroyo Collection
1104 Mission Street
South Pasadena, CA 91030
(626) 799-2576
www.arroyocollection.com

Artew Mission Studio
812 West Eleven Mile Road
Royal Oak, MI 48067
(248) 399-0413

Bungalow Basics
1210 First Street
Snohomish, WA 98290
(360) 568-5569
www.bungalow-basics.com

Bungalow Interiors
3225 Kavanaugh
Little Rock, AR 72205
(501) 975-1953

Cotswold Furniture Makers
2815 Peachtree Road NE
Atlanta, GA 30305
(877) 261-2017
www.cotswoldfurniture.com

Craftsman Collection
2551 Regency Road South, #101
Lexington, KY 40503
(859) 277-7500

Craftsman Collection
4600 Shelbyville Road
Louisville, KY 40207
(502) 259 9699

The Craftsman Home
3048 Claremont Avenue
Berkeley, CA 94705
(510) 655-6503
www.craftsmanhome.com

Craftsman Revival
985A Lomas Santa Fe Drive
Solana Beach, CA 92075
(858) 259-5811

The Emporium
1800 Westheimer
Houston, TX 77098
(800) 528-3808
(713) 528-3808
www.the-emporium.com

Fedde's
2350 East Colorado Boulevard
Pasadena, CA 91107
(626) 796-7103

The Gamble House Bookstore
4 Westmoreland Place
Pasadena, CA 91103
(626) 449-4178
www.gamblehouse.usc.edu

Greenwood
32 Miller Avenue
Mill Valley, CA 94941
(415) 389-5037

Hannah's Home Furnishings
1149 41st Avenue
Capitola, CA 95010
(831) 462-3270
www.hannahshomefurnishings.com

Hill House Antiques
276 South Undermountain Road
Sheffield, MA 01257
(413) 229-2374

Historic Lighting
114 East Lemon Avenue
Monrovia, CA 91016
(888) 757-9770
(626) 303-4899
www.historiclighting.com

Jeanne's Lamp & Mission Furniture
22 North Main Street
Liberty, MO 64068
(816) 781-3206

The Joinery
4804 SE Woodstock Boulevard
Portland, OR 97206
(503) 788-8547
www.thejoinery.com

The Lodge at Torry Pines Shop
11480 North Torrey Pines Road
LaJolla, CA 92037
(858) 777-6667

Michael FitzSimmons
Decorative Arts
311 West Superior Street
Chicago, IL 60610
(312) 787-0496
www.fitzdecarts.com

Munro's Furniture
2189 Lakewood Boulevard
Long Beach, CA 90815
(562) 986-5305

Munro's Furniture
1703 East 17th Street
Santa Ana, CA 92705
(714) 210-3800

Oak Park Home and Hardware
133 North Oak Park Avenue
Oak Park, IL 60301
(708) 445-3606
www.ophh.com

The Roycroft Gift Shop
31 South Grove Street
East Aurora, NY 14052
(716) 655-0571

Rupert, Charles
2005 Oak Bay Avenue
Victoria, B.C. V8R 1E5
(250) 592-4916
www.charles-rupert.com

Rustic Spirit
(866) 649-4799
www.rusticspirit.com

Voorhees Craftsman
1415 North Lake Street
Pasadena, CA 91104
(888) 982-6377
www.voorheescraftsman.com

Willow Glen Kitchen & Bath
351 Willow Street
San Jose, CA 95110
(408) 293-2284
www.willowglen.com

Textiles, Fabrics & Curtains

Ann Wallace & Friends
PO Box 2344
Venice, CA 90294
(310) 617-3310
www.annwallace.com

Archive Edition Textiles
12575 Crenshaw Boulevard
Hawthorne, CA 90250
(877) 676-2424
(310) 676-2424
www.textileguy.com
www.archiveedition.com

Arts & Crafts Period Textiles
5427 Telegraph Avenue, #W2
Oakland, CA 94609
(510) 654-1645
www.textilestudio.com

Inglenook Textiles
240 North Grand Avenue
Pasadena, CA 91103
(626) 792-9729
www.typeandstitch.com

J. R. Burrows & Company
PO Box 522
Rockland, MA 02370
(800) 347-1795
(781) 982-1812
www.burrows.com

Trustworth Studios
PO Box 1109
Plymouth, MA 02362
(508) 746-1847
www.trustworth.com

United Crafts
127 West Putnam Avenue,
Suite 123
Greenwich, CT 06830
(203) 869-4898
www.unitedcrafts.com

Wallpaper & Wall Covering

Bradbury and Bradbury Wallpapers
PO Box 155
Benicia, CA 94510
(707) 746-1900
www.bradbury.com

Burt Wall Papers
PO Box 1014
940 Tyler Street, Unit 3
Benicia, CA 94510
(707) 745-4207
www.burtwallpapers.com

Carol Mead Design
www.carolmead.com

Charles Rupert
2005 Oak Bay Avenue
Victoria, B.C. V8R 1E5
(250) 592-4916
www.charles-rupert.com

J. R. Burrows & Company
PO Box 522
Rockland, MA 02370
(800) 347-1795
(781) 982-1812
www.burrows.com

Trimbell River Studio and Design
PO Box 568
Ellsworth, WI 54011
(715) 273-4844
www.trimbellriver.com

Trustworth Studios
PO Box 1109
Plymouth, MA 02362
(508) 746-1847
www.trustworth.com

Victorian Collectibles Limited
845 East Glenbrook Road
Milwaukee, WI 53217
(414) 352-6971

Houses, Sites & Organizations

Boettcher Mansion (1917)
900 Colorow Road
Golden, CO 80401
(303) 526-0855
mansion.jeffco.us.

Bryn Athyn Cathedral
900 Cathedral Road
Bryn Athyn, PA 19009
(215) 947-4878
www.brynathyncathedral.org

The Charles Rennie
Mackintosh Society
Queen's Cross Church
870 Garscube Road
Glasgow, Scotland G20 7EL
44 (0)141-946-6600
www.crmsociety.com

Craftsman Farms
2352 Route 10 West, # 5
Morris Plains, NJ 07950
(973) 540-1165
www.stickleymuseum.org

Dana-Thomas House (Frank Lloyd
Wright: 1904)
301 East Lawrence Avenue
Springfield, IL 62703
(217) 782-6776
www.dana-thomas.org

El Alisal (designed and built by
Charles Fletcher Lummis:
1887–1910)
200 East Avenue 43
Los Angeles, CA 90031
(323) 222-0546

El Hubbard Roycroft Museum
(1910 Craftsman bungalow built
by the Roycroft workers)
363 Oakwood Avenue
East Aurora, NY 14052
(716) 652-4735

Fair Lane (designed for Henry Ford
by William H. Van Tine:
1913–1915)
4901 Evergreen Road
Dearborn, MI 48128
(313) 593-5590
www.umd.umich.edu/fairlane

Fonthill and The Moravian
Pottery and Tile Work
East Court Street
Doylestown, PA 18901
(215) 348-9461
www.mercermuseum.org

The Francis W. Little Living Room
(Frank Lloyd Wright: 1903)
The Metropolitan Museum of Art
1000 Fifth Avenue
New York, NY 10028
www.metmuseum.org

The Frank Lloyd Wright Home
and Studio (Frank Lloyd Wright:
1889–1909)
951 Chicago Avenue
Oak Park, IL 60302
(708) 848-1976
www.wrightplus.org

The Gamble House (Greene and
Greene: 1908)
4 Westmoreland Place
Pasadena, CA 91103
(626) 793-3334
www.gamblehouse.org

George East Ohr
Arts and Cultural Center
136 G. E. Ohr Street
Biloxi, MS 39530
(228) 374-5547
www.georgeohr.org

The Glessner House
(H. H. Richardson: 1885–87)
1800 South Prairie Avenue
Chicago, IL 60616
(312) 326-1480
www.glessnerhouse.org

Greystone
648 Wick Avenue
Youngstown, OH 44502
(330) 743-2589
www.mahoninghistory.org

The Grove Park Inn
(decorated and furnished by the
Roycrofters in 1913)
290 Macon Avenue
Asheville, NC 28804
(800) 438-5800
www.groveparkinn.com

The Historic Adamson House and Malibu Lagoon Museum
23200 Pacific Coast Highway
PO Box 291
Malibu, CA 90265
(310) 456-8432
www.adamsonhouse.org

Hotel Pattee
1112 Willis Avenue
Perry, IA 50220
(888) 424-4268
(515) 465-3511
www.hotelpattee.com

House for an Art Lover (Charles Rennie Mackintosh: designed 1901, constructed 1989–1996)
Bellahouston Park
10 Dumbreck Road
Glasgow, Scotland G41 5BW
44 (0)141-353-4770
www.houseforanartlover.co.uk/

Hull House (founded by Jane Addams in 1889)
800 South Halsted Street
Chicago, IL 60607
(312) 413-5353
www.uic.edu/jaddams/hull

John Wingate Weeks State Historic Site (built as a mountain lodge in 1916)
PO Box 104
Lancaster, NH 03584
(603) 788-4004
www.nhparks.state.nh.us/Parks Pages/Weeks/Weeks.html

The Lanterman House (Arthur Haley, 1915)
4420 Encinas Drive
La Cañada Flintridge, CA 91012
(818) 790-1421
www.lacanadaonline.com/lanter-manhouse

The Marston House
(Irving Gill: 1905)
3525 Seventh Avenue
Balboa Park
San Diego, CA 92103
(619) 298-3142
(858) 292-0455
www.sandiegohistory.org/main-pages/locate3.htm

The Mission Inn
Foundation & Museum
(Arthur Burnett Benton: 1902–1908)
3649 Mission Inn Avenue
Riverside, CA 92501
(909) 788-9556
www.missioninnmuseum.com

Morse Museum of American Art
445 North Park Avenue
Winter Park, FL 32789
(407) 645-5311
www.morsemuseum.org

Jerry and Phyllis Mattheis
520 East Church Street
Cambridge City, IN 47327
(765) 478-5993

Overbeck Pottery Museum at the Cambridge City Public Library
33 West Main Street
Cambridge City, IN 47327
(765) 478-3335
www.overbeckmuseum.com

Pewabic Pottery
(1903–1961, founded by Mary Chase Perry Stratton)
10125 East Jefferson
Detroit, MI 48214
(313) 822-0954
www.pewabic@pewabic.com

The Pleasant Home Mansion
(George Washington Maher: 1897–1899)
217 South Home Avenue
Oak Park, IL 60302
(708) 383-2654
www.pleasanthome.org

The Purcell-Cutts House
(William Gray Purcell: 1912, open the second weekend of each month by reservation)
2328 Lake Place
Minneapolis, MN 55405
(612) 870-3131
www.artsmia.org/unified-vision/purcell-cutts-house

Ragdale
(Howard Van Doren Shaw: 1896)
The Ragdale Foundation
1260 North Green Bay Road
Lake Forest, IL 60045
(847) 234-1063
www.ragdale.org

Red House (Philip Webb: 1859, designed for William Morris)
Red House Lane
Upton Bexleyheath, Kent, England
DA6 8JF
www.friends-red-house.co.uk

The Robie House (Frank Lloyd Wright: 1908)
5757 South Woodlawn Street
Chicago, IL 60637
(708) 848-1976

The Rookwood Pottery Restaurant
(Rookwood Pottery, 1880–1960)
1077 Celestial Street
Cincinnati, OH 45202
(513) 721-5456

Saarinen House (Eliel and Loja
Saarinen: 1928–1931)
Academy Way
39221 Woodward Avenue
Bloomfield Hills, MI 48304
(248) 645-3000

The Sun House and Grace Hudson
Museum (George Wilcox: 1911)
431 South Main Street
Ukiah, CA 95482
(707) 467-2836
www.gracehudsonmuseum.org

The Swedenborgian Church
(A. Page Brown: 1894)
2107 Lyon Street
San Francisco, CA 94115
(415) 346-6466
www.sfswedenborgian.org

Taliesin (Frank Lloyd Wright:
1911 and 1925)
Highway 23
Spring Greene, WI 53588
(608) 588-7900

The Friends of Dard Hunter, Inc.
PO Box 773
Lake Oswego, OR 97034
www.friendsofdardhunter.org

Wellington House (designed by
Ward Wellington in 1922)
7262 Genesee Street
Fayetteville, NY 13066
(315) 637-3155

The William Morris Society
Kelmscott House
26 Upper Mall
Hammersmith
London, England W6 9TA
(020) 8741-3735
www.morrissociety.org

The front cover and pages 50, 51 (upper), 52, 53, 59 (upper), 66 (lower and middle right), 67 (left), 105 (upper), 129, 130 (upper left), 131 (numbers 1 and 3), and 159 by Ray Stubblebine.

Pages 9, 18, 25, 26, 28, 29, 30 (right), 34, 35 (lower—with Andre Chaves), 36, 37, 41, 42, 44 (upper), 46 (lower), 47, 48, 54, 55, 56, 57 (lower), 60 (lower), 61, 62, 63, 64, 65, 66 (lower and middle right), 69, 70 (number 5), 71 (lower), 79 (upper), 80, 82, 83 (upper), 84, 86 (middle and lower), 87 (lower), 88, 89, 90, 91 (lower), 94, 96, 98, 101 (lower), 105 (lower), 106, 107 (number 1), 108 (upper right), 110, 111, 112, 113, 114, 115, 116, 117, 118, 122, 124, 125 (left), 126, 127, 130, 131 (number 4), 135, 138, 139, and 149 by Bruce Smith.

Pages 10, 11, 119, 120 (lower), 121, by Tim Street-Porter.

Page 12 by Edward R. Bosley.

Pages 16, 17, 78, 93, and 102 (number 1) by Thomas Heinz.

Pages 32 and 75 by Tim Arvin, courtesy of JAX Arts and Crafts Rugs.

Page 38 (upper) courtesy of George Hunter.

Pages 43, 44 (lower), 45, 46 (upper), and 49 (upper) courtesy of Craftsman Farms.

Pages 49 (lower) and 51 (lower) courtesy of Turgeon-Rust Collections, The Roycroft Shops, Inc.

Page 57 (upper left) courtesy of Carol Mead.

Pages 58, 125 (right), 134, 136 (upper left and right), and 137 by Tom Engler.

Pages 59 (lower) and 136 (lower), courtesy of Dimitri Shipounoff Collection, Berkeley Architectural Heritage Association.

Pages 66 (upper right), 70 (numbers 1–4), 72 (lower), and 73 (lower) courtesy of the collections of Timothy Hansen and Dianne Ayres, Arts and Crafts Period Textiles.

Page 74 (right) and back cover by Bill Erlich, courtesy of Blue Hills Studio.

Pages 76, 77, and 155 by Douglas Keister, courtesy of Bradbury and Bradbury Art Wallpapers.

Pages 79 (lower) and 81 (lower) by Jon Yost, courtesy of Raymond Tillman.

Page 87 (upper) by Randell Wright.

Page 95 by Fred Speiser, courtesy of Jaap Romijn.

Page 97 by Dennis Griggs, courtesy of Mack and Rodel.

Pages 99 (upper) and 100 by Eric Gardner, courtesy of Wood Classics.

Page 99 (lower) by Joyce Oudkirkpol, courtesy of Debey Zito.

Pages 101 (upper) and 102 (number 2) by Janis Wild, courtesy of Debey Zito.

Page 102 (number 3) by James Ipekjian.

Page 103, courtesy of L. & J. G. Stickley Company.

Page 104 (lower) by Dean Powell, courtesy of David Hellman Craftsman.

Page 107 (number 2) by Bill Schilling, courtesy of A. K. A. Drake Custom Furniture.

Pages 107 (number 3) and 108 (lower) by Jerry L. Anthony, courtesy of Paul Kemner, Furniture Craftsman.

Page 131 (number 2) by Robert Walsh.

Back flap by Timothy P. Gates.

An original kitchen in a Craftsman home. Kitchens at the turn of the century tended to be open and large, efficiently designed in order to simplify the housework. As Stickley once wrote in his Craftsman Homes, *"The very first requisites are that it should be large enough for comfort, well ventilated and full of sunshine, and that the equipment for the work that is done should be ample, of good quality, and, above all, intelligently selected."*

A home in the Bungalow Heaven neighborhood, Pasadena, California.